# THE CHURCH UNBOUND

*In that day Israel shall be a third part with Egypt and Assyria, a blessing in the midst of the earth which Yahweh of hosts blessed, saying, "Blessed be my people Egypt, the work of my hands Assyria, and Israel my inheritance."*

Isaiah 19:24-25

*A HUMAN CHURCH IN A*
*HUMAN WORLD*

# THE
# CHURCH
# UNBOUND

By Norman K. Gottwald

J. B. LIPPINCOTT COMPANY
PHILADELPHIA AND NEW YORK

To My Mother

# PREFACE

THIS study aims to find clues for a proper working relation between church and culture by looking closely at the relation between Israel and the nations in biblical terms. It is the contention of the author that a number of familiar church-culture interaction-patterns emerged in ancient Israel, which have had profound influence on all later Jewish and Christian thought. It is further claimed that these patterns require serious re-examination and reconstituting if the church is to be creatively responsive to our age.

In *All the Kingdoms of the Earth. Israelite Prophecy and International Relations in the Ancient Near East* I have spelled out some of the prophetic patterns concerning international relations. The intent here is to formulate a broader thesis and to include within it not only secular politics (the relation of church to nation) but also, for want of a better term, ecumenical politics (the relation of church to synagogue and of church to other religions). In particular, I have tried to catch the nuances of the dialectic between the church's opposition to culture and its appropriation of culture.

My intention throughout is to be completely true to the biblical evidence viewed with the strictest possible historical understanding, and at the same time to contribute to clarifi-

7

cation of the present church-culture crisis. There is a biblical
—even an ancient Israelite—way of looking at church-culture
interaction which, while not exhaustive or self-sufficient for
our purposes, can be highly suggestive and deeply determinative for a current approach to church-culture problems.

NORMAN K. GOTTWALD
BERKELEY, CALIFORNIA
APRIL 1966

# CONTENTS

9

# ABBREVIATIONS

IB    The Interpreter's Bible
ICC   The International Critical Commentary
IDB   The Interpreter's Dictionary of the Bible
LXX   The Septuagint or Greek translation of the
      Old Testament

# INTRODUCTION

A LITTLE more than three thousand years ago a new reality appeared articulately in human affairs. It has been attracting, tantalizing, and offending men ever since. It is a reality that can be stated in a simple sentence: God is in living fellowship with man. But it is a reality that can scarcely be exhausted in a lifetime or even in the span of history. Yet for many of us it is the most compelling clue to the meaning of human life and thought that has appeared to date.

The Bible, and especially the Old Testament, is the initial record of the ever renewed people in fellowship with God, a people frequently perplexed but steadily held by him, never resting but rejoicing in the movement of life which is the actual sphere of God's action.

Particularly crucial to our understanding of this phenomenon is the fact that the fellowship of God and man of which the Bible speaks is not superimposed upon human events and meanings but lies folded and entwined within them. We shall look at some of the earliest recorded moments when that reality was sharply experienced and our specific angle of approach will be the relation between the experience of God and all other human experience.

Since we are dealing with written products of the earliest biblical community, in large measure ours must necessarily be a literary and historical study. In the last analysis, however, it is a spiritual inquiry. We wish to discern the inner spiritual structure of the Israelite apprehensions of God and man, of church and world; furthermore, we wish to relate those understandings to our own. What is there in these primal records that can point us toward a fuller fellowship with God? And how are we to grasp that fellowship in relation to all the other human experience which communion with God does not negate but seeks to fill full?

We propose then, in effect, to study the relation between church and culture in ancient Israel, even though the verbal forms in which the polarity is expressed in the Old Testament are chiefly "the people [of God]" for Israel or the proto-church and "the peoples or nations [of the earth]" for the political and cultural structures and bodies outside Israel, which formed the world or culture at large.

The plan of this book is threefold. In Part I the outlines of the biblical concept of "church" and "culture" are sketched. The emphasis is on the ancient Israelite traditions, notably the prophetic, but the Mosaic foundation-faith is examined as well as some late Jewish and early Christian views. With that as background, Part II turns to four literary and theological "images" or "models" of the relation between church (Israel) and culture (the nations). The four images, one from the book of Exodus and three from the book of Isaiah, are examined in their original contexts and their primary features are analyzed as persisting elements in the biblical interplay between church and culture. In Part III the structural elements of the ancient Israelite church-culture relationship are brought to bear on the current church-culture encounter. The sense in which Israel can properly be treated as the protoype of the modern church and synagogue

12

is considered. The ancient Israelite church-culture concepts are examined for the light they throw on the relation between the church and other religions and between the church and the nations. Finally, the interaction of the church's faith, its own distinctive culture, and the wider culture are explored.

Although it is best to let the conclusions follow from the text rather than to attempt to summarize them here, it does seem wise to offer a brief account, in advance, of the chief terms used throughout. Such clarification seems all the more urgent because the terms used have been given widely varying meanings in recent biblical, sociological, and theological studies.

*People* is used to refer to the community of men from Moses to the present day who have experienced, confessed, and attempted to live out the reality of communion or covenant with God. It designates Jews and Christians. It entails both the primal personal and communal root experience as well as the consequent forms of worship and communal order, the laws and mores developed within historic Jewish and Christian bodies. It embraces a quality of faith and a pattern of life.

*Synagogue* refers to the people in its postbiblical Jewish forms.

*Church* may simply mean the people in its Christian forms, but it may also serve inclusively to represent both the Jewish and the Christian covenantal confessions.

Synagogue and church exhibit the same polarity of radical covenantal experience and communal forms that is expressed by the term "people." Naturally the use of synagogue and church as species of the one genus "people" presupposes definite views about the relation between Judaism

13

and Christianity, which will be explored more fully in Part III. For the moment it may simply be stressed that the continuity of the experience of the covenanted people may be seen in all forms of ancient and modern Judaism and Christianity. Occasionally, in order to underline the obvious fact that the ancient Israelite covenantal community was not historically the same as its later Jewish and Christian progeny, we will speak of this ancient community as the proto-church or as "church" (in quotation marks).

*Peoples* designates "natural" communities which have not experienced or tried to order themselves by the special Jewish or Christian apprehensions of God. It refers in biblical contexts mainly to other political and cultural entities (e.g., Egypt, Assyria, Babylon, Philistia, Moab). In the broad sense, however, it is employed in this study for all social, economic, political, and religious groups and structures that form the distinctive culture of man.

*Culture* denotes the total human tradition with its plastic and adaptable forms, all that man has built upon his natural and biological heritages. It is often used in this study in counterpoise to synagogue and church but never in simplistic opposition. In fact, the contrary is true, for this book aims to show that the people of God in synagogue and church must always live in consciousness of the total cultural tradition on which it draws and with which it is in contact. This means that the church *possesses* a culture of its own and *confronts* a surrounding culture. It is in the dynamic and variable three-cornered relations and tensions among the church's faith, the church's culture, and the general culture that the church faces its greatest theoretical and practical challenges. The church is only "a third part" with culture in the interests of God.

14

# PART I

# CHURCH-CULTURE INTERACTION IN BIBLICAL THOUGHT

In this section we will trace some aspects of the development of the motif of God's people in their various cultural environments during the biblical period. Attention is devoted first to the Mosaic traditions and to the pre-exilic prophets, then to the prophets of the exilic era, and finally to some instances of later Judaism and early Christianity, namely, the Dead Sea sect and Jesus of Nazareth.

Many additional facets and nuances of the particular exemplars chosen could profitably have been studied. Furthermore, other biblical cross-sections could have been examined. The emphasis falls heavily on the Israelite period through the Babylonian exile. This is largely due to the fact that the four images to be explored in greater detail all belong to this period, but the choice of period and images is not arbitrary. It is the author's conviction that the fundamental church-culture interaction-patterns of subsequent Jewish and Christian experience were already clearly set forth, and at least partially elaborated, by the sixth century B.C. The brief selective synopses of Qumran and Jesus are intended chiefly to show the endurance of the earlier patterns and the manner in which they were modified, added to, and developed.

# A. MOSAIC AND
# EARLY PROPHETIC TRADITIONS

It is totally impossible to understand the teaching of the
first writing prophets unless we take into account the prior
work of Moses. This is not to say that the body of traditions
about Moses was completed by the time of Amos, for it was
not; nor is it to say that there are no problems in recovering
the actual work of Moses, for there are many. It is simply to
say that the prophets stood firmly upon the covenant traditions and understood themselves not as founders but as reformers. They believed that the norms of Israel's life and the
motive power for obeying them sprang from the holy events
of God's revelation when Israel was formed in the womb of
Egypt and brought forth into the wilderness and the land
of Canaan. If our purpose were to focus upon the entirety of
the Mosaic traditions, then a host of historical questions
would at least have to be touched upon. But for our purposes, namely, to discover the roots of the prophetic notion
of the people of God, we shall take the traditions as they
were known to and imbibed by the prophets. This means
that we shall focus on the earliest Mosaic traditions (the so-
called JE portions of the Pentateuch) in sketching the preprophetic notion of church and culture.

Integral to the call of Moses and the deliverance of Israel
from Egypt is the intimate connection between God and

people, which is apparent in a wealth of phrases: "my people who are in Egypt" (Exod. 3:7); "that you may bring forth my people" (3:10); "Yahweh,[1] the God of your fathers" (3:16); "Yahweh, the God of the Hebrews, has encountered us" (3:18). A frequent formula used by Moses in addressing Pharaoh in the name of God is: "Let my people go, that they may serve me" (Exod. 7:16; 8:1, 20; 9:1, 13; 10:3).

Of particular pertinence for the Mosaic understanding of the people of God is the introduction to the revelation at Sinai:

You have seen what I did to Egypt, and how I lifted you on eagles' wings and brought you to myself. Now, if you will fully obey me and keep my covenant, you shall be my prized possession from among all the peoples; for I possess all the earth, and you shall be my kingdom of priests and a holy nation.

(Exodus 19:4-6)

This passage will be analyzed in Part II as the first of four major images. For the moment it is sufficient to underscore two basic thoughts in the passage: the first is Israel's unique relation to God, as a prized possession, an unusually valuable treasure. Yet Israel's role is not an inert and passive one, for she is in covenant, bound as a vassal to the King of the world.[2] The second leading notion is that Israel's favored position is not asserted to the exclusion of other peoples. Negatively stated, Israel's salvation does not jeopardize the salvation of the nations. Positively stated, Israel exists as a body of priests on behalf of the nations. This second theme is not highly developed, and is even obscured by the bitter struggle of Yahweh with the Egyptians and by the arduous task of forming the slave rabble into a responsible people. Yet the tension is posited between Israel's distinctness from

18

and Israel's identification with the world. The distinctness of Israel was always in danger of being misunderstood when her original and continuing connection with the peoples of the earth was forgotten.

The centrality of the people of God in the thought of Moses could be developed at far greater length. In his intercessory prayer for the apostates who have made the golden calf, he asks for assurance of God's abiding presence: "For how shall it be known that I have found favor in your sight, I and your people? Is it not in your accompanying us, so that we are distinct, I and your people, from all the other peoples that are upon the face of the earth?" (Exod. 33:16). And in the Song of Moses:

> When the Most High gave to the nations their inheritance,
>   when he separated the sons of men,
> he fixed the boundaries of the peoples
>   according to the number of the sons of God [LXX; Heb.,
>     "Israel"].
> But Yahweh's portion is his people,
>   Jacob his designated heritage.
>
> (Deuteronomy 32:8-9)

The same theme could likewise be traced through the writings of the conquest period, in clearly preprophetic portions, e.g., in the Song of Deborah with its recital of the triumphs of "Yahweh, God of Israel" through "the people of Yahweh" who wage war in his behalf:

> . . . there they sing forth the vindicating acts of Yahweh
> the vindicating acts of his peasantry in Israel.
>
> (Judges 5:11)

Again, the role that Israel is to play toward the other nations is obscured by the struggle to occupy the land and by a rather too simple conviction that Israel's enemies are God's enemies. It is nevertheless clear that God makes use of the other nations, who are also his, in order to chastise his faithless people.

All in all, the preprophetic notion of the people of God includes them under a special protection and a special obligation. They hold title to the land on condition of obedience. Cultus (formal religious practice) and ethics (relations among men) are included in the obligation. The preservation of Israel, sharply punished and purged, is essential to the pledge of protection. The traditions centering in Moses are preserved as the special property of the tribal league which formed a loose confederacy worshiping a common god but retaining tribal autonomy.[3] In other words these preprophetic traditions of the people of God preceded the monarchy. In them the king is immaterial to the Law. It is indeed striking that the Old Testament contains no royal law. Law is regarded as stemming from the premonarchic period, from the period of tribal confederacy.

Over against the nonroyal matrix of covenantal faith must be set the fact that the great writing prophets were all prophets under monarchy or in the wake of monarchy. Monarchy created new tensions to which prophecy spoke as the religious conscience of Israel. In keeping with Israel's fundamentally religious outlook, the newly adopted kingship had been given Yahweh's sanction. Prophecy sought to keep that sanctioning in check, to qualify it at the point of responsibility before Yahweh—not by asserting individual worth of citizens as such but by asserting the priority of God's election of Israel over the election of the king. This trend is stronger in some prophets than in others but the drift is clear: kings are subservient to Yahweh, to *torah*, i.e., to the instruction of prophet and priest. Hosea is even able to conceive of the obliteration of kingship altogether and a return to the desert. Isaiah, at the other extreme, anticipates the rise of a king wholly righteous in whom justice and power perfectly coincide.

A prior commitment and responsibility to Yahweh is invoked by the prophets as binding in all the areas of Israel's life, in spite of its growing complexity and impersonal character. In agriculture and commerce, as in statecraft, the old Mosaic spirit of common loyalty was insisted upon by the prophets as the condition of Israel's welfare as God's people. In other words, each of the realms of Israel's life, as it became more complex and demanding, had tended to develop its own spirit—a spirit that seemed remote from Yahweh. Israelites had come to feel that political, economic, and social self-advancement were their essential aims in life. They pursued such ends fervently.

The prophet insisted that for the people of God all political, social, and economic pursuits stood under divine sanction. They must measure up to the revelation of cultic and ethical obligation. Thus the abuses and problems the prophets treat are monarchic, but the God in whose name they speak and the loyalty they exact are largely drawn from the old tribal confederacy and its traditions of deliverance from Egypt and of the covenant at the mountain. Yet that thundering God of old was Lord of the land and of this crucial time as he had been Lord of the times of deliverance and covenant. All times and places are alike his, who is Lord of culture, notwithstanding that the center of revelation for the prophets is in the creation of a people by him who is Lord of the "church." The burden of their complaint was that Israel was not currently being the people of God. Their concern for the future was how God would revitalize his people.[4]

Amos held that the people of God had defaulted through negligence of ethics, through falsification of the covenantal foundation of Israelite life—not through openly rejecting the covenant but through a practical disregard of it. Life was really being formed on some other basis than fidelity to God and fellow Israelite. It was being formed on the basis of self-aggrandizement in terms of Canaanite religious, political, social, and economic standards. The detailed indictments of the book of Amos must be seen within two frameworks: (1) the Canaanite structure of civilization accepted by Israel within which were few ideological restraints upon unlimited self-attainment through force or guile; and (2) the Mosaic-Israelite structure of covenantal brotherhood in which the drive toward self-attainment was balanced and fulfilled within a community of responsible selves under divine law.

Amos re-emphasized the neglected twin in the covenant union of privilege and obligation. "Only you have I known / of all the families of the earth, // consequently I will punish you / for all your iniquities" (Amos 3:2).

Amos seems largely to think of the people of God as identical with the citizenry of the kingdoms of Israel and Judah. He entertains no certain notion of how God's purpose is to be continued without the wicked kingdom. There is brief allusion to a remnant, "it may be that Yahweh, God of hosts, will be gracious to the remnant of Joseph" (Amos 5:15), but "remnant" here does not have moral and spiritual import; it simply means the survivors. In the impending judgment Amos expects that the righteous will fall with the wicked; for evil has waxed great and the kingdom has suffered moral rot beyond the point of remedy.

Amos rigorously restated Yahweh's total demand on his people as well as his sovereign independence of Israel. The seriousness entailed in being God's people, the absolute necessity of embodying and reflecting God's character, is forcefully advanced. He removes any doubt that being God's people is simply a natural or sociological fact, as it was in other ancient Near Eastern religions. Being God's people was a condition demanding continual appraisal and renewed dedication. The divine purpose stood above Israel and called Israel to a vocation higher than she would have chosen on her own. Amos thus poses the intolerable tension between Yahweh's demand and Israel's defection, between a lofty religious ethic and a rawly selfish mode of life that affected pompous religious poses. Prophecy thus sharply formulates the issue between true faith and pseudo-religion, between a genuine church-culture polarity and a facile culture-religion.

HOSEA follows in Amos' tracks; his indictments are equally severe, though slanted more toward political and cultic infractions than toward social sins. Where he goes beyond Amos is in the greater measure of hope that he holds out for the people of Israel, though he can hardly be called sanguine in his expectations. He apparently sees repentance following probation. He personalizes the relation of God and people in terms of the husband-wife imagery, but the demand for right relations is fully as urgent as in Amos and in some ways even more so owing to the emotional force of the imagery. The divine jealousy, with Yahweh conceived as an enraged husband or as an aroused she-bear, is vividly expressed. He will have his way with what is his; yet the jealousy of God is ultimately controlled by love. God's hasty impulse to destroy is checked by his calmer second thoughts:

> How can I give you up, O Ephraim!
> How can I surrender you, O Israel!
> . . . . . . . . . . . . . . . . . . . . . . . . . . . . . .
> My heart recoils within me,
>   my compassion grows warm and tender.
> I will not execute my terrible anger,
>   I will not again destroy Ephraim;
> for God am I and not man,
>   the Holy One in your midst,
> and I need not come to destroy.
>                           (Hosea 11:8-9)

The ways of Canaan have been misleading ways for Israel, particularly in agriculture, which was so tied up with the religious notions of the baals as the owners of the fields and the guarantors of fertility. Hosea is also extremely impatient with the political order—or rather, disorder. Kingship was appealing to weak and unprincipled men. The new civilization has led to apostasy, but Yahweh is till master and sponsor of civilization. Yet because Israel has not recognized that fact, a reversion to the old tribal system, to desert simplicity, may be inevitable. Such a probationary period, a kind of spiritual quarantine, would perhaps bring Israel to her senses. As Yahweh's wife she would pledge herself in new vows of undying matrimonial love.

The quality most needed in the people, but at present most lacking, Hosea describes as the knowledge of God, an insight into the divine nature, and thus a desire and capacity for obedience to Yahweh. Nothing can replace such understanding; the social fabric decays without it, for knowledge of God is the fountainhead of the ethical life as it is also virtually a synonym for life with God. To know God is to know one's own good and the good of one's fellows. Soundness of state and society depends upon this hallmark of God's people: knowledge of God, fellowship and rapport with him, sensitivity to what Yahweh is and therefore what Israel must be.

By the same token Hosea is conscious of sin as an accumulating weight upon the man or people who turns from knowledge, ultimately as an enslaving power. For Amos there are sins; for Hosea SIN. Amos sees sinners who could repent but through habit will not; Hosea sees sinners who will not repent because they cannot—they are in bondage of will.

Thus Hosea leaves us before the dilemma of God's love that requires Israel's salvation and Israel's bondage in sin that requires her rejection. The note of ultimate salvation appears to prevail but how the impasse is to be broken through and the chasm spanned is not apparent to Hosea, although he does not feel that political defeat and exile are inconsistent with this final victory of love. His nostalgia for better days comes close to cultural primitivism, but in the end Hosea concludes that the full life of the "church" is possible only in the contemporary culture. But such a life is possible only for a repentant and revivified church.

ISAIAH OF JERUSALEM at his call expected "a root-and-branch" judgment on the sin of Israel and Judah. He had little hope of being widely heard. For several years prior to his call Isaiah had doubtless noted the hostile and indifferent reception given Amos and Hosea in the northern kingdom. Why should he expect better response in the south?

In spite of his gloomy inaugural charge, an emphatic note of hope for the future of God's people recurs in the genuine oracles of Isaiah. Wherever we meet this hope its essential feature is that of a minority who become the bearer of God's purpose. Even among his vehement denunciations in the style of Amos there is an interesting proviso:

> Therefore says the Lord,
>> Yahweh of hosts,
>> the Mighty One of Israel:
> "Ah, I will recompense my enemies,
>> and avenge myself on my foes.
> I will turn my hand against you
>> and will smelt away your dross as with lye
>> and dispose of all your alloy.
> And I will return your judges as at the first,
>> and your counselors as at the beginning.
> Afterward you shall be called the city of righteousness,
>> the faithful town."
>
> (Isaiah 1:24-26)

Isaiah's most characteristic expression for this purified minority is "the remnant." His first son was named Shear-jashub, "a remnant shall return." Although there are difficulties in the text in 8:16, 18, the prophet appears to speak of his family and close disciples as just such a loyal minority. Although Ahaz will not follow the life of faithful trust for the state urged by Isaiah, at least that word of faith can be kept alive within a smaller circle. Just how this group of the continuing faithful was related to those who might be shocked into repentance by impending disasters is uncertain. Perhaps he expected that the inner circle would be enlarged through additions as more and more Israelites came to their senses.

Isaiah has often been described as the initiator of the idea of the church: that is, a nonpolitical body of believers. This distinction must be applied, however, with caution; for he did not openly reject theocracy with its identification of church and state. He, rather, believed that this theocracy

26

was best represented in the faithful remnant and, if chapters 9 and 11 are Isaiah's—or at least traditional materials which he respected—he looked for a new king to arise whose righteousness would permit the state to fulfill its theocratic destiny.[5] Strictly speaking, Isaiah's notion of the remnant was not sectarian. He did not favor withdrawal from Israel. Yet he clearly differentiated between faithful people and faithlessly distorted institutions, and thus decisively between church and culture.

Whatever the prophet himself intended, his followers came to apply this element of hope to the city of Jerusalem following its spectacular deliverance from the Assyrian army of Sennacherib in 701 B.C. (Isa., chaps. 36-39). This miraculous sparing of the city contributed to Jerusalem's elevation and glorification as the sacred city. Zion's radiant transformation as the redeemed city became the subject of numerous later additions to the message of the original Isaiah. The equation of the city and its inhabitants with the remnant was vigorously rejected by Jeremiah a century later, notably in his famous Temple Sermon (Jer., chaps. 7 and 26).

Isaiah's stress upon faith sharply set off the function of the people of God in an insecure world from every other sociological or political grouping. It is his reliance upon God as Lord of the world that leads the prophet to an active interest in world affairs and yet at the same time stirs him to trenchant criticism of Israel's participation in the power struggles of his day.[6] Assyria was understood by him as God's rod of punishment but Assyria was herself proud and ambitious and unconscious of the divine purpose in her successes. Isaiah sees a hand stretched out over all the nations. The political neutrality urged by Isaiah upon Ahaz and Hezekiah is based on a bedrock trust which reached far below the superficial collective security arrangements of the nations. Being the people of God, even though living in the world, Israel must rely upon the Holy One of Israel. She cannot have recourse to one standard as a believing community and to another standard as a nation. As the visible people of God she must live by the sacrifice and patience demanded by God.

Perhaps stated in more modern terms we would say that Isaiah understood national sovereignty to be subservient to higher ends than that of the state itself. His counsel of neutrality is based not upon political irresponsibility but upon a deeper sense of obligation to Israel's purpose. National independence did not take precedence over the religious obligation of God's people. There was another kind of independence—the independence of a people established in the divine holiness and righteousness. Nations weak and mighty, fearful and haughty, must come to see that there is a higher will that rules in their affairs. God's people have the mission of living by this truth, even if it appears to leave them defenseless and exposed to the ravages of other nations.

For the most part, the pre-exilic prophets equated the people of God with the empirical or visible Israel. They warned of severe and virtually total judgment in the light of Israel's election to special responsibility. Their concern was almost wholly ethical rather than cultic, except insofar as thoughtless indulgence in cult was an ethical issue. They stood apart from Moses in their having to deal with Israel's life in the advanced civilization of Canaan with its institutions of monarchy, agriculture, commerce, and urban life. There were reservations about the possibility of mixing

Yahwism and higher civilization, as in the cases of Micah who regarded the cities with dark suspicion and of Hosea who had no love for the kingship, at least as he knew it. In the main, however, they see the coping of God's people with new circumstances of corporate life not only as an inevitability but as the only pathway to maturity in faith. They are anything but simple reactionaries or primitivists who mournfully pine for the good old days.[7] They insist, rather, that the spirit of old, the Mosaic ethos, the essentials of the blood brotherhood be retained in the more complex circumstances. The law codes are largely post-Mosaic attempts to spell out some of the concrete terms of such casuistry whereby the old spirit could be newly embodied.

But so far had God's people strayed, so serious were the inroads made by Canaanite ways of thinking and acting, that from Amos on there are reservations about the empirical Israel satisfactorily bearing her commission as God's people. The only solution Amos can see is radical judgment. Hosea, beginning from the other side, sees that God's faithful love demands the existence of a people, yet the means whereby "not my people" are to become "my people" are hardly clearer to Hosea than they were to Amos. Isaiah is the first to assert with any consistency that an integral part of God's proceeding with his people is to treasure up and preserve the faith of a few who benefit the many. The remnant is Israel in embryo. This remnant is to trust in trustless days, to be calm in chaos, and await God's new deed. Isaiah's conception of the remnant is not doctrinaire; it is a purely practical conception. The remnant is simply those few who obey Yahweh, some of whom were in the prophet's immediate following, others of whom were yet to be awakened to obedience in the turmoil of the times.

The eighth-century prophets thus begin with the awful awareness of Israel's dereliction as a people, a fact which leaves them stunned; by the end of the century they are beginning to see that it is their task to stand in the breach along with all whom they can convince, and literally to be the people of God until the whole Israel is awakened to its task. They occupy a representative position and are faced toward Israel in anticipation of the revival of faith and mission in those who by their legacy from Moses are the covenanted people. This early prophecy sees a serious disjunction between church and culture but it does not forsake culture; it seeks to build a church-consciousness so vital that it can keep its bearings while living in and adapting to various cultures.

## B. LATER PROPHETIC TRADITIONS

JEREMIAH and Ezekiel have been included among the exilic prophets even though the ministry of the one was almost totally prior to 587 B.C. and of the other in large measure before that time. The reason is that they are both harbingers of the new life beyond disaster; their message was adjusted to the age of exile and particularly to the conditions under which Judaism could survive exile. When not speaking to exiles they addressed virtual exiles.

JEREMIAH, who appears one century after Isaiah, shares with his eighth-century predecessors many features, especially the poignant image of Israel as the wife of Yahweh, the memory of a period of desert faithfulness broken by apostasy in the land, and the tragic power of sin to warp and corrupt the moral instincts and the capacities of choice. He carried the insight into sin even further, for he saw it as a deep-seated corruption of the human heart. He relentlessly exposed the incorrigible self-deception of man and prayed with fervor that his own weaknesses be forgiven and transcended by Yahweh so that his prophetic mission would not be ruined by false motives, such as envy and vindictiveness toward his uncooperative fellow Jews.

Doubtless the chief contribution of Jeremiah was a ready grasp of Israel's need for revitalization at the grass roots. We speak of him customarily as "the prophet of individual responsibility," which means really not the dissolution of the collective character of Israel but, rather, the reassertion of Israel through the wholehearted assent of its members. He saw that if Israel were to continue as the people of God, individual Israelites would need to develop a new maturity and resourcefulness. Shortly, with the fall of Jerusalem, they were to receive little tangible encouragement to retain their identity as believers in the God of Israel. In fact all the encouragement would be in the other direction: to desert Yahwism in favor of the gods of the conquerors. It is essential that Jeremiah's supposed "individualism" not be mistaken for a religion of the inner man in the sense of free thought and individual opinion, as though each Jew were complete in himself and a law unto himself. He still stood in community, but that community was now utterly dependent upon the rebirth of a common conviction. Men would have to be Jews, worshipers of Yahweh, for a reason. The prophet saw both the welfare and the obligation of the individual and of the group as fully coincident. Consonant with this inner assent as the ground for the outer cohesion is Jeremiah's expectation of the removal of all visible cultic supports and symbols, at least those that had been most treasured: the king, the temple, the ark, the sacrificial system.

Yet the visible Israel remained as a newly motivated people. Jeremiah's notions of what shape the people of God would take after Judah's fall are complex and not entirely integrated. At least four elements appear:

1. He looked to the reunion of the northern and southern kingdoms (Jer., chaps. 30-31), an expectation which was by no means wholly utopian, since the Jewish governor ap-

pointed by the Babylonians at Jerusalem's fall, namely Gedaliah, ruled at Mizpah and may have had authority in southern Samaria as well as in Judah (chap. 40).

2. He saw the exile in Babylon as a constructive process, purgative and educational in its effect upon the exiles. They were to be the "basket of good figs" in contrast to "the badly spoiled figs"—that is, those who clung to Palestine in disbelief that the exile was more than a brief aberration in Judah's continued political progress (Jer., chap. 24). His famous letter to the exiles in chapter 29 reads like the charter of Judaism through these 2,500 years since he wrote: "Seek the welfare of the city to which I have exiled you and pray to Yahweh on its behalf, for in its welfare you will discover your welfare." (29:7).

3. He expected the reconstruction of Palestine (chap. 32). The symbolic action in which he buys the field from his cousin Hanamel, even while the siege is in effect, is interpreted by him as an act of hope and of trust in the future of God's people in the land: "For thus says Yahweh of hosts, the God of Israel: Once again houses and fields and vineyards shall be bought in this land" (32:15). If this be eschatology, it is most decidedly earthbound!

4. He looked for the new covenant (Jer. 31:31-34), which was in fact a recovenanting ceremony of the sort specified in the book of Deuteronomy and apparently observed in the old tribal league at such central sanctuaries as Hebron and Shechem.[8] Yet Jeremiah contributes a new dimension—an inner directedness that transforms the whole relation of God and people into spontaneity, into liberation from *law as compulsion* to *law as the principle of self-realization.* However, this new covenant must not be misread as Christian interpreters have sometimes done, as though each man

33

now has his own access to God as an individual apart from the group. To say this is to attribute to the ancient prophet the atomistic individualism of rationalism and romanticism in modern Western thought. Note carefully how the terms of the covenant read: "I will make a new covenant with the house of Israel and the house of Judah . . . and I will be their God and they shall be my people." (31:31, 33).

The covenanting parties are Yahweh and his people; each man knows Yahweh through a perfect assent, that is an utterly free affirmation of his membership in the people of God. Again we should have to say in terms of modern categories that the thorny problem of individualism and collectivism is overcome in the new covenant where every man becomes wholly himself as he affirms his identity in Israel as a member of the people of God. In place of the former false collectivism in which men abdicated their true individuality by obeying the law as compulsion or else throwing it off in pursuit of other gods—the gods of culture and nationality—they will now be able to address a common center and be determined by it, yet in utter freedom, in complete selfhood. Thus will the ancient promise to Moses be realized: "I will be their God, and they shall be my people."

EZEKIEL's prime function was to interpret the exile positively in an even more concrete fashion than Jeremiah was able to do. The preservation of the people is taken for granted, as was true of prophecy from Isaiah on, but now only as a sheer act of grace. Israel deserves nothing but reprobation; yet for his own honor Yahweh will preserve his people: "that you or they [either Israel or the nations] may know that I am Yahweh." The "everlasting covenant" that God established with his people no longer gives the illusion of being upheld by Israel. It is solely God's act that there

34

should be a people at all. This motive of divine self-vindication, of the humiliation of Israel to the point of complete self-emptying of pride, the surrender of any claim upon God, must not be forgotten when we turn to Ezekiel's concern with individual responsibility.

His attitude toward God's ways with Israel, his theodicy, if you will, assumes then the right of God to do as he chooses, considering how repeatedly wayward Israel has been. Yet the other aspect of his vindication of God is to show that God's moral judgment is not mechanical arbitrariness, for He does not treat the present body of exiles as solely the products of previous sin. To be sure, they are the evil issue of the harlot Judah. But they are more, for the people God creates are not merely an inert workmanship, in spite of the impressions that Ezekiel sometimes makes in this regard. They are not simply like an artist's product or even like a sign merely pointing to or away from God. They have an inner life of their own in responsibility to God so that the lines of responsibility from the past, the consequences of former sin, do not disallow the present responsibility. This is the point of Ezekiel, chapter 18, which elaborates the thesis that "the person who sins shall die." Men "live" or "die" in their choices and not out of necessity. Clearly Ezekiel has not now dissolved God's people as an entity; he has, rather, newly established its responsibility. Being a member of God's people, however much it binds one with other men past and present, does not rob the individual of his freedom to live either in fidelity or infidelity to God's will. Unfortunately Ezekiel is an extreme example of the lack of system or of qualification and subtlety in prophetic thought and expression. The prophets were dialecticians who dealt with the paradox of the relation of God and man, but their method of thinking and writing was suited rather to single urgent monolithic emphases rather than to balanced statements.

But the prophets were after all whole men and we must try to see into the paradox by which they lived even if they have not framed it in a clear and balanced fashion. Ezekiel at any rate sees that peoplehood does not mean mass anonymity; it is not an absolute notion that could relieve each Jew of his own free decision. God was resolved to have a people and his promise would hold, but just what place each believer was to have in this community depended very greatly upon his own response. The exiled Jew must not think of himself as a free agent dissociated from the people of God since he is caught in the consequences of the past; this point would scarcely have been overlooked by the Jews who had heard the prophetic interpretation of the ills that had befallen them. Yet God held before them a significant range of decisions that either advanced or retarded their participation in the fellowship of God's people. The terms "live" and "die" seem to contain this dialectic; they are not mainly biological in reference, but refer to quality of life, to the wasting away of life or to its augmentation.[9] While the people as a totality were wasting away, "dying" in exile (compare the vision of the valley of dry bones, chap. 37), within this communal decline "life" was possible, and not as a mere memory but as a present reality; in fact life could increase through the free decision to live under God's will. While Ezekiel's forms of expression on the matter are neither so aesthetic nor so precise as Jeremiah's, the point is the same: membership in God's people does not rob a man of freedom or of the responsibility that calls him to

36

reverse the general trend of decline and death with an increase of obedience and therefore of life.

The poet-prophet of the exile who, for want of a better term, we call ISAIAH OF THE EXILE, opens his epic poem with the cry: "Comfort, comfort my people" (Isa. 40:1). We may be very sure from the tone of his writing that the spiritual desolation and futility of exile evidenced already in Ezekiel had by his time (a generation or more later) worked further havoc. The very notion of Israel as God's people was highly problematic. As a surviving folk idea, a nostalgic tradition out of the past, it might be worth preserving for the sake of cultural cohesion. But the old dynamic of a covenant corporateness was seriously undermined. The crucial role of this prophet was to give contemporary theological and cultural grounding to Israel as God's people, lest it cease to have any identity except as a backward-looking sociological entity, a Palestinian fossil, a church encapsulated in an archaic culture or, at the opposite extreme, absorbed into Babylonian culture.

This is the basis for his so-called pronouncement of full or explicit monotheism. Either Israel has to do with the sole and sovereign God or else religion is just another pastime that can as well be exchanged for some other and the many gods themselves become interchangeable and optional. But since Yahweh is the sole sovereign God, Israel has an unqualified relationship to him and an unqualified obligation to open an access to Yahweh for all the nations. Thus the Lordship of Yahweh over creation and history is asserted in order to strengthen Israel in her faith and awaken a sense of mission. Implicit in her faith in one God was the invitation to the nations to join his people:

37

> Turn to me and be saved
> all the ends of the earth!
> For I am God, and there is no other.
> (Isaiah 45:22)

The interpreter who seeks more light as to the basis on which the nations would be incorporated into Israel comes soon to the realization that Isaiah, chapters 40-55, is highly rhetorical poetry. It is hard to believe that a man could write with such glowing vision of the winning of the nations to Yahweh without himself being an evangelist for his cause, both among his own people and among the Babylonians. One can imagine him preaching in assemblies of Jews and see him reasoning eloquently with Babylonians. Yet the strategy, the methodology of Israel's mission is sought for in vain in the magnificent poetic tapestry of Isaiah, chapters 40-55. There is no airy spiritualization of "the new thing" that God will do because it tied up with the restoration of Jews to Palestine made possible by the Persian king, Cyrus. The prophet at times uses imagery that could be read as a description of the nations as vassal states of Israel, summoned to obedience to the restored Davidic dynasty. Yet it is extremely difficult to regard the Servant in whom the rulers of the nation behold their salvation as a king, and the unequivocal praise the prophet gives Cyrus rules out that the Jewish supremacy would be politically expressed. Cyrus is in fact God's "messiah," forger of a world empire, for which Israel will be the priestly agent. The Persian political supremacy will be linked with the Israelite religious supremacy.[10]

Isaiah of the exile has at any rate pushed to the utter limits of the old covenant. Israel has ceased to be a political entity; her own destiny has been realized in her having been put to death in exile. But the enigma stands that Israel is a blind and deaf Servant and the nations have not sought Yahweh. Israel's self-sacrifice has not achieved its goal. Thus the Servant inevitably stands as an enigma (see pp. 76-86). He must be Israel and yet he cannot be Israel. But Israel is after all more than meets the eye; Israel is more than this scraggly group of exiles. It is an idea in perpetual embodiment and yet seeking further embodiment. Israel is the divine intention given instrumentality. Israel is not merely a belief; it is a spiritual fact. Thus the Christian interpretation of the Servant must accept a duality of reference in the Servant figure, namely, the literal reference to the actual body of exiles and the discrepancy between the divine intent through Israel and Israel's actual performance. Precisely here we see the naked condition of the people of God for whom the designation is something of a mockery if not ludicrous. Jesus Christ is the Servant in that he is Israel, the old and the new conjoining and rising to fruition. In him as universal promise, as the lodestone of the nations, the old Israel and the new Israel exceed themselves. But only as instruments for the fellowship of God and man just as Jesus is himself such an instrument. "There is none good but God alone" (Mark 10:18).

Thus we have seen that the people of God was the fundamental theme and the primary context of Hebrew prophecy. The focus upon this theme is as different in the pre-exilic and exilic situations as was Israel's experience. In the eighth and seventh centuries—and that includes Jeremiah and the early Ezekiel—the threat to true peoplehood is the superficial optimism of a culture religion. The reverse of being God's people was a kind of easy identification with social, political, economic goals which were given religious sanctions by means of Yahwistic approval. Amos, Hosea, and Isaiah thus had to deal with those who had no difficulty regarding themselves as God's people as long as this meant the people who are favored by God with tangible bounty. In the sixth century, however, the threat to true peoplehood was meaninglessness: doubt of God's goodness and power and thus in a realistic sense practical atheism that doubted God as the center of Israel's existence. Whereas previously the theocentric orientation of Israel was taken superficially, it was now under a total and radical question. Those to whom Jeremiah and Ezekiel spoke after 587—and especially those among whom Isaiah of the exile lived after an extended exile, marked by religious and cultural rootlessness—were uncertain in what sense, if at all, they could be God's people.

The one danger in this situation was that Yahwism might be retained as a folkway, a whitewash hiding the charnel house within, a decoration on the bleak façade of political death. Jeremiah, Ezekiel, and Isaiah of the exile are all at pains to show that God's purpose is broader than the old cultic order. There is no going back for Israel to any kind of cultic substitute for total allegiance, for the true turning of life around the axis of faith and obedience. Though they disagree as to the role that cult will play in the restored community (Ezekiel, for example, allowing a large place to the new temple), they are at one in finding no meaning for this cult structure outside of the everlasting covenant and the bond of God and man. Either Israel must get hold of her central purpose and of her essential precariousness as God's people, accept the life of faith and obedience, minister to the nations; or else she must surrender Yahwism as a pretense. But of course they did not see Israel in a final cul-de-sac, because God's promise was that he would always have a people. They could not conceive an end to the people of God, and thus again and again fire was stirred in the ashes of Israel!

The people of God is thus seen to be a notion and reality in one sense at odds with culture, in tension with Israel's tendency to substitute contemporary forms of life for allegiance to God, either in her naïve nationalism or in her chastened disinheritance. Yet though she has clutched culture at times boastfully and at other times bitterly, it is fundamental to the prophetic notion and reality of the people of God that Israel live in a culture and express God's sovereignty in the existing patterns of life. Fundamental to all phases of the prophetic conception of God's people is the impulse, one might almost say necessity, to find expression for the divine will, to corporealize it in a body of men. The old Mosaic tensions of obligation and privilege, of separation and mission remain indelibly written on the prophetic memory. But the great question remains: How is God to break the vicious circle of apostasy and failure in accord with his promise? If Israel does not give up her individuality, how can all the nations be God's? If Israel does sacrifice her distinctness, where will be the locus of God's peoplehood, where will its center be? The dilemma becomes almost intolerable in postexilic Judaism where the one center that seems capable of holding together, namely, Israel's obedience to the Law, is also the wall of separation and offense to the nations. Has the purpose of God's people indeed come to nothing?

"Church" for these prophets could never be an isolated segment of past culture venerated in the present. "Church" if it were to mean anything, had to be the living nucleus of fellowship and meaning in the midst of contemporary culture, drawing strength from and throwing light upon man's common life.

# C. QUMRAN AND
# NEW TESTAMENT TRADITIONS

THIS section is sharply restricted to a few salient points at which the Dead Sea community and the New Testament faith share the older biblical tradition and to a few points of contrast between them. There is no intention to sketch the history of the sect,[11] or to survey its literature,[12] or to discuss the identity of the Teacher of Righteousness; [13] nor is there need to trace the idea of God's people through the entire New Testament.[14] While the treatment will be considerably more cursory than the exposition of the prophets, with the Mosaic-prophetic backdrop and with the relation of the Qumran sect to the early church in mind, the Christian conceptions of church and culture will be seen in sharper perspective.

The Qumran sect was a strictly disciplined reform movement in Judaism; it was in fact a sect which believed that in the constituting of its membership Israel was being "reformed," i.e., formed again and formed properly. "All the brethren were Jews, but all the Jews were not brethren." [15] Sect members took upon themselves an oath to obey the laws of Moses and to live by the community Rule. They had no single name for themselves but employed a wide variety of titles: "covenant" (berîth), "congregation" ('ēdāh), "assembly" (qāhāl), "council" ('ēṣāh), "community" (yaḥad), "many" (rabbîm).[16]

Closely allied with its separatist spirit was the sect's view of the Jewish priesthood. The sectarians were "sons of Zadok" of the priestly line tracing its ancestry back to one of the priests installed by David. This line of succession had been ignored by the Hellenistic appointees to the priesthood and also by the Maccabeans who became priest-kings from 140 B.C. on. In the absence of a valid priesthood in Jerusalem, the Dead Sea "sons of Zadok" claimed to offer the only valid worship at their cloistered settlement in the desert. In their meals they celebrated the only acceptable sacrifice and they observed festivals according to their own calendar. They were the faithful bearers of the true Israel until such time as God would manifest himself in judgment and vindication. Those not within their ranks would be destroyed. They were the exclusive Israel of God.

Supporting this belief was the Qumran sect's sharply dualistic view of the two Spirits created by God to control all human history. Each man's "lot" consigns him to the jurisdiction of one or the other of the Spirits: the Spirit of Perverseness or the Spirit of Truth. "Between the two categories He has set an eternal enmity." [17] After an allotted period of struggle, the Spirit of Perverseness and the sons of darkness will be overthrown and the Spirit of Truth along with the sons of light will prevail. The end is shortly expected. The Qumran sectarians anticipate that in the imminent time of triumph "a Prophet will arise" like Moses (cf. Deut. 18:15-19) and also two messiahs will appear, the Messiah of Aaron and the Messiah of Israel.[18] In other words, the roles of prophet, priest, and king will be filled in the moment of God's victory.

Scripture is interpreted in terms of the violent events precipitating the birth of the sect, its persecution and imminent triumph. The Teacher of Righteousness, while not himself a figure of the New Age, is an interpreter of the New Age. He illuminates the Scripture by reading its references to God's people as references to the sect he has founded. The familiar commentary style of Qumran accords with the sect's belief that all Scripture was written to point to these last things. Thus by a kind of typology the prophets can be truly understood as alluding to culminating sectarian events, e.g., the voice in the wilderness (Isa. 40:3), the cornerstone (Isa. 28:16), and the booth of David (Amos 9:11).

How does this sectarian interpretation of God's people compare with the ancient prophetic view? In both there is a serious concern for the purity of Israel, i.e., for Israel's faithfulness to its basic constitution, to the purpose of its creation. This purity is understood less dynamically by the sect than by the prophets. The sectarians are most like Ezekiel in their juxtaposition of moral and ritual purity on a par. This does not make them in any sense solely or self-consciously dependent on Ezekiel. The sectarians share, rather, the late Jewish concern for total moral and ritual obedience, which Ezekiel had so profoundly influenced and which the reforming work of Ezra and Nehemiah had furthered.

The Qumran covenanters were distinguished above all by being a true sect that had ceased to believe in Israel's capacity to fulfill the conditions of salvation. The sect members had no more mission to apostate Israel except to hold out the invitation of membership to those few who would receive it, presumably by divine "lot." In this they are at sharp variance with all the prophets who were unable to surrender at least a measure of hope for Israel. The prophets never

45

severed their connections as citizens of the communities in which they belonged, whether as members of the kingdom or as exiles.

The prophets, as we have recognized, were deeply disturbed by the general failure of Israel to be God's people, by an ethical and cultic failure that was at heart a theological failure: a failure to accept life under God. They condemned and grieved for the wayward and negligent majority. Somehow its role must be assumed by the minority who will be faithful and obedient. The prophet is thus aristocratic in his thinking; he speaks of a remnant, or of the exiles as a basket of good figs, or of the Suffering Servant. He believes in redemption by the aristocracy of the faithful. Yet these conceptions are not ultimately restrictive; the minority is not closed so that it can never again be enlarged. It is not in quest of its own salvation to the exclusion of the majority. Its minority status is not exclusive but representational; it exists to restore the large covenant community to God's purpose and, with the Servant, that covenant community is potentially the world.

The sectarian dualism of Qumran, so rigidly adhered to, is foreign to the flexibility of the prophets. The prophets were looking for fulfillment of God's purpose within the orders of this world. The sectarians were looking for the abolition of this world. Both in its withdrawnness from the world and in its exaggerated dualism, the Dead Sea sect develops a conception of God's people considerably different from that of the prophets, while nonetheless drawing upon prophetic writings and images.

Where does the early Christian conception fit in relation to the prophets and to Qumran? [19] Common to them all is the concern with the perpetuation of the true Israel, in other words, the consummation of God's will among men. Jesus shared much of the late Jewish apocalyptic dualism which puts him closer to Qumran than to the prophets. His ministry may be understood as the formation of a quasi-sectarian movement that demanded repentance, change of life in the light of the imminent end. He may also be seen as a free interpreter of the Old Testament in the light of current happenings, seeing in his own work and the activity of his little band of penitents and disciples the fulfillment of prophecy: ". . . and beginning with Moses and the Prophets he interpreted to them the things concerning himself . . ." (Luke 24:27). There is an unmistakable sectarian flavor to the church founded by the historical Jesus.

The similarities between Jesus and Qumran are by no means the whole of the matter, nor even the heart of the matter. There is a countercurrent in Jesus' thought and action that is indicative of the old prophetic tension between Israel separated and Israel sent.[20] Jesus did not withdraw into ascetic retreat. The new Israel was formed in the midst of the old. Immediate results might be meager indeed as a result of the preaching of his little band; but God's intervention would bring victory on a far wider scale. While Gentiles were not openly sought by Jesus, he saw intuitively that repentance and faith would secure for them a place in the Kingdom; he could even envision men from east and west sitting down to eat with the patriarchs in the Kingdom of God (Matt. 8:11).

Jesus also showed a greater freedom toward the Law than did the Qumran covenanters who in fact were even stricter than the Pharisees. The Dead Sea sect, for example, forbade saving an animal from a pit on the Sabbath, which Pharisaism allowed. A far freer relationship of persons in love and faith—typical of the old Mosaic and prophetic theme—was allowed for, indeed demanded, by Jesus than was the case at Qumran. Jesus regarded love as the ultimate power not only among believers—which of course all Jewish groups believed—but significantly toward outsiders and evil ones; and he acted consistently on that conviction.

Yet to say all this does not remove the apocalyptic dualistic elements from Jesus' teaching. Jesus expects the end of history with even more intensity than the Qumran group. He sees the end as present in his ministry: "If I by the Spirit [or finger] of God cast out demons, then the Kingdom of God has come upon you" (Matt. 12:28; Luke 11:20). Furthermore, there is much evidence that Jesus regarded himself as the delivering figure incognito, whom he preferred to identify as the Son of Man. His cleansing of the temple and reinterpretation of the Law are doubtless to be thought of as messianic acts, that is, acts belonging to the New Age and to the proper prerogatives of himself as the initiator of the New Age. Yet the chasm between the now and the then, between the weak and failing little band of followers and the gathering in of the nations to the Kingdom of God, is not easily crossed. The victorious denouement of history remains for Jesus a mystery of God's great love and power.

Historically it can be said, therefore, that Jesus combines *prophetic vision and depth* with a *sharply modified sectarian dualism*. The elements of freedom and universalism in his outlook were to be seized upon and given new implementation by the Gentile wing of the church and especially by Paul. But the church was never able to forget that its triumph in the world is still a mystery, a triumph that awaits the strange, sometimes convulsive and sometimes gradual moving of God's Spirit.

God's people are thus not merely the people favored of God but the people appointed of God, marked by his character, and driven into the world to fulfill his purposes. Jesus and the first Christians were open toward culture, however tentatively, in a way that Qumran covenanters were not. The church of Jesus is sown as a sect of faithful Jews; it will be harvested as a wider company of Jews and Gentiles.

## PART II

# FOUR IMAGES OF CHURCH-CULTURE INTERACTION IN ANCIENT ISRAEL

# A. THE CHURCH
# DISTINGUISHED FROM CULTURE

## *Exodus 19:2b-6* *

Israel camped there before the mountain and Moses ascended
to God and Yahweh called to him from the mountain saying,

> "Thus you shall say to the house of Jacob / and declare
>    to the sons of Israel, // [1]
> 'You have seen what I did to [or "in"] Egypt //
> And how I lifted you on eagles' wings / and brought
>    you to myself. //
> Now if you will fully obey me / and keep my cove-
>    nant, //
> You shall be my prized possession from among [or "in
>    preference to"] all the peoples; / for I possess all the
>    earth; //
> And you shall be my kingdom of priests / and a holy
>    nation.'"

SOME twelve centuries before Christ, several hundred or
several thousand Semitic-speaking people fled from Egypt
to escape intolerable social and political conditions. Their
leader had the Egyptian name Moses. The people came to
be known as Hebrews or Israelites and eventually as Jews.
Spiritually we are all Jews. Whatever it was that began then
was in an important sense our own beginning.

We wish that we knew far more about the previous his-

* Related passages: Gen. 12:1-3; Exod. 33:12-16; 34:6-10; Deut. 7:6-8;
9:4-5; 14:2; 26:16-19; Isa. 61:5-7; Matt. 3:8-9; I Pet. 2:4-10; Rev. 5:9-10.

tory of those people, about their origins, their language, customs, and religion. We wish that we knew the circumstances of their life in Egypt, of their flight, and of their experience in the desert to the east of Egypt. Most of what we know is fragmentary and until 150 years ago was confined strictly to what the Bible reports. The modern recovery of the ancient world has thrown considerable indirect light on the events of Israel's birth. The general outlines of the biblical report seem plausible, although much of the detail is questionable, having undergone the kind of simplification and exaggeration which characterizes legend.[2]

We could profitably discuss several features of the accounts in the first five books of the Old Testament: the identity of the Pharaohs, the plagues in Egypt, the route of the departure from Egypt, the crossing of the sea or marsh, the camping places in the desert, the manna and the quail, the location of the holy mountain, the religious shrine composed of a portable tent and boxlike ark, the collections of law.[3] But that is not our purpose here. After all these historical and religious features are explored, the central persisting fact in the traditions is a people who felt itself delivered by God from oppression in Egypt and brought into unique fellowship with him in the wilderness. There was the initiating exodus and there was the consolidating covenant. Even if we should take a very dim view of the historical actuality of those events, the fact is that later Israelites and Jews and Christians believed that they and their ancestors were delivered and covenanted with by God. Whenever and however the belief arose it appeared as an eruptive and astonishing conviction. Often misunderstood and corrupted, violated and despised, the reality of the communion of Israel with God has persisted.

54

In the book of Exodus, and by foreshadowing in the book of Genesis, we first encounter the persisting and disruptive historical reality of Israel as the proto-church or people of God.

Exodus 19:2b-6 contains one of the earliest reflections on the reality of the people of God. It is a poetic passage placed in the story at the point where the refugees have reached the mountain of God, Sinai-Horeb. It is presented as a direct word of God to the people. It is not easy to assign the passage to any of the classic pentateuchal sources with confidence. It has marks of belonging to the so-called Elohistic or northern (E) source of the books of Moses.[4] The phraseology is, however, in some respects closest to the Deuteronomic (D) source familiar to us in the book of Deuteronomy.[5] And features of the Yahwistic or southern (J) source are even distinguishable.[6] The date for the passage may be anywhere between 950-550 B.C. in its written form, and in its oral form it may easily go back to the period of the judges.

The thing that strikes us first in this passage is its poetic form, the successive lines dividing in typical Hebraic poetic fashion into members or half-lines that are in parallel with one another. The language is penetratingly imaginative. It is the condensation of much reflection on the meaning of the flight from Egypt and the covenant at the mountain. It is the distillation of experience in the way that creeds and prayers are distillations of experience. Nothing is wasted or superfluous.

It is, in short, a confession of faith put in God's mouth. It is not, strictly speaking, Israel confessing but God announcing to Israel his purpose with Israel. In that sense it reminds us of the promise to Abraham in Genesis 12:1-3,

55

which is a foreshadowing of the promise to the whole people of Israel. And we are reminded further of another confessional cry put into the mouth of God in Exodus 34:6-7 where, as God passes by Moses on the mountain, he intones:

Yahweh, Yahweh, a God merciful and gracious, slow to anger, full of steadfast love and faithfulness, maintaining steadfast love for thousands, forgiving iniquity and rebellion and sin, but who will by no means clear the guilty, bringing the iniquity of the fathers upon the children and the children's children, to the third and the fourth generation.

And in the same context, after Moses has confessed the sin of his people and asked for pardon, God continues:

Behold, I make a covenant. Before all your people I will do marvelous deeds, such as have not been previously done in all the earth or in any nation; and all the people among whom you live shall see the work of Yahweh; for it is an awesome thing that I will do with you.

(Exodus. 34:10)

The fact that the confession and promise recorded in Exodus, chapter 34, is from the earliest source of the books of Moses, dating perhaps in the tenth century B.C., strengthens our impression that theological reflection upon Israel's beginnings of the sort contained in Exodus 19:2b-6 was a very ancient practice.

At any rate we can now appreciate that the trenchant poetic confession of Exodus, chapter 19, belongs to the atmosphere of worship, the adoration and praise of God. We must think of it as spoken and intended in the sense of a call to worship, a summons to thanksgiving, a confession of obligation. It is neither historical document nor theological treatise in the limited and proper senses. It is liturgy, service to God. It is Israel's origin and destiny seen

56

as only worship can see the whole *sub specie aeternitatis* ("under the aspect of eternity").

The thing that overwhelms us in the confession is Israel's acute awareness of being a people in the midst of the nations and yet unlike the other nations. She is a nation but a holy nation, i.e., a nation dedicated to her God. She is a kingdom but a kingdom of priests, i.e., God is her King and she is the priestly mediator for the other nations. She is marked as his, indelibly and irretrievably, beyond all recall or evasion.

Following the covenant ceremony, Moses is shown in his deep discouragement and desolation as the leader of Israel and the mediator between God and Israel, so that he cries out:

"Now, if I have really found favor in your sight, show me indeed your ways, that I may know you so as to gain your approval. Consider that this nation is your people." And he said, "My presence will go with you and I will give you rest." And he said to him, "If your presence [literally, "face"] will not go with me, do not send us up from here. For how shall it be known that I have found favor in your sight, I and your people? Is it not in your accompanying us, so that we are distinct, I and your people, from all other people that are upon the face of the earth?"

(Exodus 33:13-16)

Moses urgently seeks an assurance that will be adequate to his task. He must know God's plans; he must have an assistant; he must behold God's glory and know his name.[7] But in all these endeavors he is disappointed. The only consolation is God's presence and this presence is seen in his going with Israel; Israel's distinction is precisely and only that God goes with her.

It is easy to be unimpressed, even offended, by such a view of God. Is this really the novel reality at the root of

57

synagogue and church? That God singled out some ancient Semites and honored them? It is a most unlikely promise and method. What horrors Jews and Christians have practiced, sometimes on one another, in the name of that loveless doctrine of election. Should we not as quietly as possible put this barbarous and distorted belief to rest?

Should we not say that God has no people as such, merely individual favored persons? Or, should we not say that his people are all nations? Perhaps we can affirm both claims, but not too hastily, not in order to negate the first fact that stands emphatically in our past and impinges repeatedly on our present: God has a people in this world who are among the nations but also over against them, not to be confused with any of them. If the old doctrine must go, it goes not by denial but by being caught up in its fulfillment. The people must be there among but distinguished from the nations if individuals are to find satisfactory life and if the nations are to be fulfilled.

The people of God, Israel, is God's specially valued treasure, his heirloom, his cache, his obsessive delight. From out of and in preference to all peoples he chooses this people. What an incredibly narrowsighted and arbitrary God—a joker, fiend, or senile old fool! Can this be the God of the earth and of all men upon it, who plays games with men and showers gifts on his favorites?

Yet at the heart of the confession is the reminder, "For I possess all the earth." Israel will not be permitted to forget that all the peoples and nations are his making. Creation as a developed doctrine is fairly late in Israelite belief, but as an experienced reality it is at least as old as the early story of creation in Genesis, chapter 2. Yahweh is not a god bound to choose this or that people, or any people. He is not the god of blood and soil. He is over all peoples and over all lands. Only such a nongod can be God.

What God has done he has done with deliberation, and the people chosen as his special treasure must respond with deliberation. They must know that the possessor of all the earth, the caller forth of the nations, wants a kingdom of priests and a holy nation. And the astonishing thing is that he wants this people for the sake of the world, for the benefit of all nations, as is declared in the promise to Abraham: "For in you all the earth's families will be blessed or will bless themselves" (Gen. 12:3).

If God wants all nations blessed why does he not bless them all directly? Why the devious method of a special people? Why the agony and struggle of human history when God could manifest himself directly and fulfill all heart's desires? Or could he?

How much easier to turn from such tormenting questions to the simple enjoyment of being God's people, of being Israel, of being the church. God loves us and all is well! It is reasonably logical if he loves us because we have been good or at least better than others—and so we subtly reshape the confession until it reads: "Then you shall be my prized possession among all the peoples / for you are the upright upon the earth!"

And in that moment the people of God are cut off from their origin and from their destiny. They are cut off from God and they are cut off from the nations—cut off from the two foci of their life, the two realities they are intended to bring together. They cease to be conductors and become barriers. Against this all too natural and all too logical conclusion stands the firm word: "For I possess all the earth."

The passage still does not say in what way Israel can exist

59

for the nations. No Bible passage tells us really how this can be so. But experience teaches us much if we will heed it; we know that all life depends upon other life, that one person mediates grace or judgment for others. One and all, we men are caught up in a great movement whose meaning cannot be known until it is all acted out. But we have been told ever since Moses, and especially since Jesus Christ, that the formation of a people among the nations will be for the incalculable blessing of the nations, that the few must be gathered in order that all may be perfected.

Yet the superhuman mystery and our own resistance to it persist in jolting juxtaposition. Enigmas arise on every hand. God not only wills the salvation of the nations but he terrorizes and destroys them. So the confession begins: "You have seen what I did to [or "in"] Egypt." A curious way to will the salvation of Egypt, to curse and to destroy it. Yet could it really be that Egypt is hurt that it may be healed, that the nations are humbled that they might be lifted up?

The people who are formed by the rescue from Egypt, the people brought to God at the mountain, are not left merely to contemplate God's mysterious election and then freed to enjoy his favor. Their conduct has not made them the people of God but their conduct will be forever marked by their being the people of God. "And now if you will fully obey me and keep my covenant. . . ." What an awesome *if!* The truly impossible *if!* The grace of God precedes and includes the *if* of Israel's response, but the *if* remains in force.

This God meets his people in their common life and awakens their full obedience. How tempting it is to equate that obedience with human rules and ideas, for obedience would be an empty illusion without the stuff of human life, without actual words and deeds. The books of Moses teem with compilations of directives and models for conduct which at many points resemble those of other nations.[8] The common life of all the nations is a life to be lived by the people of God, yet they must live it without believing that in any of these rules and practices God's will is exhausted or trapped.

The awesome *if* will not disappear. Every segment of life is a place for obedience. We are consumed by demands for obedience, and only the knowledge of his presence can transform the *if* from threat into promise, and from death into life.

How frivolous and frustrating to live by a bundle of principles and codes instead of by the presence of God. Yet how idle and vacuous to think that God's presence can be anywhere but in just these obligations and relations that make up the life of the world. The holy nation is, therefore, not the perfect nation conceived as the total keeping of a set of rules; the nation is holy, rather, in its direction, the way its life is pointed, what it looks for, what sights and sounds and hopes and fears it catches up out of its environment and lives by.

And so the people stand in the midst of the nations and yet distinct from them. All too often, the notions which this truth has released in history have been idolized, trivialized, and bastardized. Any one element taken by itself, frozen into a system or a slogan, grasped as a last straw, hammered into a false god may become grotesque, preposterous, and demonic. In the name of God godless things may be believed and done, and Jews and Christians have believed and done them. Even the living generation of the church is not exempted.

61

But the truth lives in spite of all its corruptions. The reality reasserts itself at every level of our experience. When we have fled to the most profane nations and categories of experience, and presumably found a hiding-place from religion and theology, in all those activities and roles which bespeak vulgarity and commonness, suddenly we find God's people; we are overtaken by a priestly word or deed that recovers life, that brings forgiveness and grace. Even where no religious language has been used, a shaft of God's grace penetrates and transforms. We know that the Bible has not contained him. He is here, at our side, in our hearts.

Very early in its inception this belief in a people of God was a sophisticated and subtle thing in the sense that those who lived by it were sensitive to its dangers and corruptions. They knew what a fine line the people have to walk, how narrow the way really is, how comforting it is to turn God's people into a religious or ethnic society, celebrating its goodness and reveling in its own habits and values.

To be God's people then is to be split, split between all the easy identities of the world and the one identity of a called people. To be God's people is to participate in the nations and in all other social and political groupings and yet not to belong finally to any of them, to be a people enroute to some higher purpose which cannot be readily defined but can be sensed and described in the fellowship of men wherever wholeness is restored.

It is an ultimately indefinable and preposterous notion. It is clear that it cannot be tested finally short of the end of human history itself. But having seen one of the earliest stages of the appearance of this belief we are struck with what maturity and power the idea appeared, what agony and exaltation it caused men then as now, and what splendid and intimate companionship we find with these ancient men who used another language and lived by different customs and mores but who prove to be our brothers on the way.

# B. CULTURE
## ATTRACTED TO THE CHURCH

### *Isaiah 2:1-4; Micah 4:4* *

The word [or "happening"] which Isaiah ben Amoz saw concerning Judah and Jerusalem:

"And it shall occur at the end of the days /
    that the mountain of Yahweh shall be secure //
On the summit of the mountains, /
    and it shall be exalted on the heights; //
And all the nations shall flow to it, /
    and many peoples shall go up to it. //
And they shall say:
'Come and let us ascend to the mountain of Yahweh, /
    to the house of the God of Jacob; //
That he may teach us his ways, /
    and that we may walk in his paths.' //
For from Zion shall go forth instruction, /
    and the word of Yahweh from Jerusalem; //
And he shall judge between the nations, /
    and he shall reprove many peoples; //
And they shall hammer their swords into plowshares, /
    and their spears into pruning hooks; //
Nation shall not lift sword against nation, /
    nor shall they continue to learn war. //
But they shall sit, each under its own vine, /
    and under its own fig tree, and none shall disturb
        another." //
For the mouth of Yahweh of hosts has spoken.

* Related passages: Isa. 9:2-7; 11:1-9; Isa. 10:5-16 + 14:24-27; 12:4-6;
17:12-14; 29:5-8; Isa. 14:28-32; 18:1-6; Joel 3:9-15; Isa. 42:1-4; Matt.
8:10-11; John 12:20-32; Acts, chap. 10.

64

THE people of God never stands still. Its task always changes as its context changes. The world of Isaiah looked decidedly different from the world of Moses.

In the latter half of the eighth century before Christ, Israel was emerging into the main flow of world history. Under David and Solomon she herself had become a powerful political force in the region between Egypt and Mesopotamia, but in the following century and a half her unity and pre-eminence were not maintained. Internally, she split apart into the two kingdoms of Israel in the north and Judah in the south. Externally, by turns various powers in Egypt and Mesopotamia, and also in Palestine and Syria proper, became stronger than either of the divided Hebrew kingdoms.

About 735 B.C. Assyria became the most powerful and consistently threatening outside force ever to appear in Palestine. Under a series of strong militaristic kings Assyria held a tight grip upon Syria and Palestine, completely extinguishing the northern kingdom of Israel and drastically limiting the freedom of maneuver of the southern kingdom of Judah.

Isaiah lived through this time of increasing external threat from 740 to 700 B.C. His was the first age when Palestine was thoroughly linked with world history. In his prophetic message, the nations—and especially the hated Assyrians—come to the fore as in no previous portions of the Old Testament. To be the people of God in that time and place meant to face the reality of the nations as a sphere of constant turmoil and of peril to national security. The world trembled and groaned, revolt and counterrevolt wracked it, punitive campaigns lacerated it, military might shaped it, and shallow patriotism swayed its emotions. One man in

Jerusalem during these tumultuous decades, as army after army swept into Palestine, talked about faith and quietness, "If you do not believe, you will not endure," (Isa. 7:9b) he said to the Judean king.

But have you ever tried to tell a king or a president, a politician or a bureaucrat to believe? To enact policy consistent with his private belief? Indifference and scoffing were Isaiah's lot when he made the preposterous suggestion that faith in God might even require the disregard of armaments and foreign alliances. When faith rules over fear all sorts of unexpected consequences follow; the full risk of being the people of God becomes apparent.

Israel was still locked in a struggle for her own soul. Was she first of all a nation like all the nations and only secondarily God's people? That is, should she take care of her military and political security first of all and then in "spiritual" matters trust in God? Or was her mission as God's people precisely to be strong so as to prevail over the heathen? Israel did not know and the church does not know; God's people has never known consistently where its first allegiance lies. The people has vacillated. Isaiah thought of people and nation as one, but he believed that a small faithful remnant would have to be purged for some future revival of the people.

Isaiah's prophecies are not entirely clear on many points. No nation or church could simply rule itself by means of them. There are topical gaps and poetic expressions. He provides no blueprint for government. He reflects, rather, a life-and-death conflict over the nature of the life and loyalty of the people of God, a people constantly in tension between life's "necessities" and God's "realities." Isaiah lives in this tension and will not let Israel forget it.

Wherever people are sensitive to their call from God, Isaiah's message will carry. Wherever domestic injustice—whether corrupt courts, racial inequality, degrading housing, spoliation of the land, coercion of conscience, idolization of the profit motive—wherever these and many other abuses appear, Isaiah's cool and bracing judgment will be felt like the wind of God among the dry bones. And wherever foreign policy is belligerent and self-opinionated, where nations put victory above truth, revenge above justice, national interest above human interest, where force becomes an end instead of a means, where nations crusade against nations and are too proud to talk or to confess a mistake, there Isaiah's cruel logic of God strikes with an awful swiftness and flame among the rotten tangle of nationalism and militarism.

The prophet saw only a measure of success in his lifetime. Having preached judgment upon Israel and Judah, he turned toward the end of his days to announce judgment upon arrogant and cruel Assyria. History was a leveling process; God has hewn the nation with his battle-ax Assyria, but now the weapon was to be broken and cast aside. Jerusalem would be besieged but she would be spared, not by Judean arms or by the slim reed of Egyptian support. No, God would spoil the Assyrians by some natural catastrophe. And though the exact circumstances are not known, Judah's independence was spared in spite of an enormous payment of tribute.[9]

But what consolation or proof was that? Assyria was still strong. Men killed and were killed. Nations boasted, rising and falling as they presumed to bless and curse others by their self-determined standards. Could one be more idealistic or naïve than Isaiah? What nation or what rational man can live by faith if faith means to disregard the laws of self-preservation?

An impasse has been reached. If God is to have a people it must somehow survive. To survive it must follow the rules of the world. Yet having survived by those perverse and ugly rules, is the people any longer recognizable? Has Israel gained one kind of life only to loose the most important quality of life? And the church, scattered among the nations, loses herself in the interests of the nations in order to survive. Having survived, she ceases to penetrate, to leaven, to revolutionize; in short, she is among the nations and one with the nations—living their proud and self-justified life— no longer standing over against the nations as the sign of the new reality that God intends for the world.

It was probably toward the end of his life that Isaiah wrote the great poem of the exalted mountain of God in Jerusalem now contained in 2:1-4. Practically the same poem appears in Micah 4:1-4. It is likely that the more original form of the words is found in Isaiah, but the version in Micah 4:4 preserves a conclusion since lost in the book of Isaiah.[10]

This brilliant oracle is fully understandable as the work of the aged prophet. In its form it is indebted to the enthronement songs of Israel's temple worship, and especially to the Songs of Zion, which picture Jerusalem and her worship of God as the center of the world.[11] Aside from the spacious thought of the poem, it has none of the telltale marks of prophecies written during or after the Babylonian exile.

The songs of enthronement in the Psalms and elsewhere in the book of Isaiah are of two types: those in which the king is the instrument of Yahweh's salvation (Isa. 9:2-7; 11:1-9) and those in which God alone acts without an intermediary (Isa. 12:4-6; 14:25; 17:12-14; 29:5-8). This belief in Zion as the center of God's revelation to the nations was probably as ancient as David's capture of the city of Jerusalem from the Jebusites (II Sam. 5:6-10). Here God could bring the nations beneath his will. Often the proclaimed submission of the nations was connected with their acknowledgment of the Judean king, the anointed one, God's appointed "son." This belief served to reinforce the confidence that the dynasty of David was the divinely appointed line of kings which might some day be honored by all the nations.

Isaiah takes up this traditional theme of the centrality of Jerusalem and develops it in a startlingly novel way.[12] Jerusalem is to be the center of the earth by persuasion instead of force. Not the victory of Davidic arms, but the appeal of Israel's teaching about God is to win the consent of the nations. The nations which have flailed one another on the threshing floor of hatred and pride will find a point of common reference in the God of Jacob. When this happens, a new phase in human history will have been initiated. The prophet says it will occur "at the end of the days," i.e., at a decisive turning point in history. He does not speak of the end of history but of a new era of religio-political confederation among the nations. This era cannot be measured by time. It awaits some awakening among the nations but it does not depend upon human perfection; it requires repentance and common consent. The nations which flow toward Jerusalem will say:

> "Come and let us ascend to the mountain of Yahweh, /
>   to the house of the God of Jacob; //
> That he may teach us his ways, /
>   and that we may walk in his paths."

Only when the nations are able to say this for themselves and to gather voluntarily at Jerusalem will the day of peace have arrived. Judah cannot compel them by force of arms. God cannot compel them by signs and wonders. They must see that Jerusalem is exalted; they must recognize that in the ways and paths of Israel's God there is justice and peace for all the nations.

It is a stirring vision. As poetic as the garb is, behind it lies a realistic understanding of what is needed for the fulfillment of man's longings for peace and order. At a minimum, the nations require a common frame of reference for settling disputes and some means for resolving differences among them. Only under such conditions can war be put aside as an instrument of aggrandizement and terror, as well as a means of rough justice in a chaotic world. Through forty years Isaiah had seen how national self-interests prevailed over truth and justice, how men who are personally humble and trustworthy, will lie and plunder for the nation. He had learned bitterly that man is a beast to his fellow man, that the pinnacle of his civilization—the empire state—is also the epitome of man's brutality and pride.

The frame of reference envisioned by the prophet is a common belief in Israel's God, the sense of a single will that rules over man to his upbuilding and to the maintenance of the many separate, just interests of nations. The means of settling differences is to be the instruction of Israel's God, the teaching offered by his prophets at Jerusalem.

They are to be the disinterested judges of disputes among the nations.

Can the prophet honestly have believed that Assyria, who mocked and despised the idols of the nations, would turn from her war-god Asshur to Israel's God of peace? Would Judah for that matter give up her cherished dream of conquering the other nations and restoring the kingdom of David? Was not the ancient bond between war and religion, between the worship of power and the exercise of power too strong to be broken? And is that bond not as firm now as ever in history, so that the function of the church is to pray while the nation bombs? It is, in short, a lovely dream of peace—but nothing more.

The centuries have come and gone, thousands of wars have been fought, every one of which has been justified in somebody's eyes. The nations have regarded themselves as ends in themselves, alone capable of judging their own interests and causes. The people of God has never been able to decide its position among the nations with respect to war. It has been sometimes eager to wage a crusade, to bear arms for God. It has occasionally stood aside and claimed no part in the interests of justice in society and among nations. More often the church or the synagogue has blessed the nations in their wars, not directly bearing arms but releasing its members to bear arms.[13]

Seemingly, Isaiah could not have been more wide of the mark. What he saw demands far too great a change in human nature and political structures to be credible in our history. Or does it?

"At the end of the days." At the end of what days? When the days of the era of Isaiah—and the prophet's era is still our era—shall have run out, then the nations will finally know that peace is the only solution to their problems. Will it be when they stare into the pit of chaos and self-destruction that they shall pull back? Can fear teach what reason has been unable to teach? Or will the slow growth of social order within nations finally reach out beyond the boundaries of the state, and institutions lock arms with institutions across national boundaries in a final confederation of the nations?

"At the end of the days." But have we many days to wait? Will the end of the days be also the extinction of life as we know it? And what will man have learned after he has destroyed himself in apocalyptic suicide? And in all this what do the people of God do besides wring their hands or put the sign of the cross or the star of David on their uniforms and weapons?

Isaiah dreams dreams and sees visions but they are dreams and visions about this world. They are so real that this world cannot live without them. They are so basic that we would give everything to make them our own. Almost everything, everything except repentance and new ways of thinking and acting.

When will the nations of which we are members say, "Come . . . that he may teach us his ways / and that we may walk in his paths"? And if they did, what would they learn? No snap answers, no evasions of those relations and obligations which mark the life of man in the world. For the warless world, with a common frame of reference and an agreed way of solving disputes, would still be a world of change and ferment.

But it would be a world learning peace. Isaiah says an unbelievable thing. He says that "nation shall not lift up sword against nation / nor shall they continue to learn war."

Nations *learn* war. War is not blind fate. It is learned. It is an instrument of social change in which many of our unconscious and unadmitted instincts find expression. Those instincts can find other outlets; war can be *unlearned*. War will not cease merely by removing weapons, but it also will not disappear by preparing for it and hoping it won't occur, nor by nations insisting that only the other nations need to change their ways. War will disappear by a series of painful steps, by laborious efforts, by making it no longer necessary or profitable. Fear may have its share in this, but the deepest contribution will be from self-insight through faith in the larger reality of mankind and of God.

The people of God will draw the nations. Isaiah even conceived of the prophets solving international disputes. This may be his biggest fantasy. Can we expect that any one religion will prevail over the others, that any body of religious leaders is wise enough to adjudicate such disputes? It would be premature perhaps to build programs on such premises, to create the machinery and to invite the nations to a parliament of religions. The nations must come. The dream of the Judaizing, or of the Christianizing, or even of the religionizing of the world is a precarious dream. The people of God will not programmatically redeem the world. The nations will come to the people of God or the nations will perish.

But what does it mean that they should come? If God creates and yearns after the nations, if his people exist to mediate his will to the nations, is it important that the people be seen and honored? Have they any beliefs or prerogatives that they must cling to as their own special gift to the world?

Could the ascent to Jerusalem and the teaching of the

prophets be the gift of God's people to the world indirectly? Can it be that the dim stirring in the nations for another way of life is the fruit of God's secret witness through his people? Could it be that peace will be won without much credit going to the church and the synagogue, and yet when the reality is assessed it will be shown that believing men and women by the thousands have contributed to the edifice of peace in their work as scientists, politicians, technicians, and teachers?

But there is no rest in such hope unless we are as articulate as possible about the people's role among the nations. We would hope that God is working among the nations not merely in spite of us or in ignorance of us but, occasionally, through us. We cannot set the terms on which the nations will come to us, but we must be clear at what points the people of God has something to say to the nations, something to say to them in the name of the Creator of the nations.

It will no longer suffice for us to be good Americans, good Russians, good Frenchmen, good Israelis, good Egyptians, good Indians, and then secondarily good Jews and good Christians with that part of us left over after the state has made its claims. The frontier between people and nation must be thrown down in all its harsh clarity. We must accept the agony of the split in our own lives. We must not numb our feelings and consciences and souls while we push Isaiah's dream into the far future.

The people of God awaits the nations but it keeps its own faith alive and it brings its own conduct beneath the judgment and mercy of God. It will not bear with the idolatrous worship of the state and its "isms," even if they are called Zionism or Socialism, Americanism or Capitalism. Even when they possess laudable aims and beneficial results, these provisional gains will not be simply equated with God's whole will for man. The church lives under the fear and love of God directed at itself as a community and directed at the nation and culture in which its members also have membership.

Above all, the church will not try to trade the agony of the nations for easy comfort in Zion.

# C. THE CHURCH
# INCORPORATES CULTURE

### *Isaiah 49:1-6* *

"Listen to me, O coastlands / and give heed, people far off! //
Yahweh called me from the womb, / from my mother's body
    he named me. //
He made my mouth as a sharp sword, / in the shadow of his
    hand he hid me; //
And he formed me as a glistening arrow, / in his quiver he
    concealed me. //
And he said to me,
  'My Servant are you, / Israel in whom I will be glorified.' //
For I said,
   'In vain have I labored, / for waste and void I have used up
     my energy; //
   Therefore, my cause is with Yahweh, / and my reward with
     my God.' //
And now Yahweh has said— / (He who formed me from the
    womb as his servant, /
To restore Jacob to him, / and to gather Israel for him, //
For I was honored in Yahweh's sight, / and my God was my
    strength) //
—Indeed, he has said,
   'It is too inconsequential that you should be my servant /
    to raise up the tribes of Jacob, /
    to restore the surviving Israelites; //
   So I will appoint you a light to the nations, /
    to be my salvation to the ends of the earth!' "

* Related passages: Isa. 42:1-9; 50:4-11; 52:13-53:12; Jer. 1:4-10; 11:18-
20; 12:1-6; 16:19-20; 20:7-12; Ps. 22; Gal. 1:15-16; Matt. 24:14; Luke
2:29-32; Acts 13:44-48; Acts 26:22-23.

SOMEWHAT more than a century and a half later than Isaiah of Jerusalem, the kingdom of Judah had lost its independence and most of the Jewish leaders were living as political prisoners in Babylonia. They had been there for forty to fifty years. Two generations had been born in exile. They had learned to accommodate themselves to a new way of life, without king or temple, largely dependent upon the ancient traditions of their people as interpreted by teaching prophets and priests.

One of these prophets was a man whose poems are collected in chapters 40-55 of the book of Isaiah. We do not know his name, or it may actually have been that he took the name Isaiah because he depended upon Isaiah of Jerusalem more than upon any other of his predecessors. It is likely that his poems were added to those of the first Isaiah because he stood in the tradition or "school" of Isaiah. He is often called the second Isaiah, but we have designated him Isaiah of the exile (see p. 37).

His poetry is sheer soaring lyricism which, along with the Psalms, is doubtless the most loved and used portion of the Old Testament. It is poetry of unbounded faith in the power and purpose of God in history. It would have been easy enough to celebrate God's ways in a time of national prosperity and victory. Isaiah of the exile speaks from the low point of the Babylonian exile. Nothing outwardly supports his confidence in God's new deeds for his people, nothing except the persistence of faith in Israel's God among an important minority of the exiles.

Through the seven centuries between Moses and the Babylonian exile, Israel had been torn between being a people of God and being a nation like all the other nations. When Nebuchadnezzar abolished the independent state of

77

Judah and deported its leaders, Israel was no longer a nation in the usual sense. Could her living heart as the people of God continue to beat without the bodily skeleton of political independence? It did. Isaiah felt the pulse and sounded ecstatically his belief that Israel lived solely because of God's marvelous grace.

The survival of the Jews in exile was exceptional. Doubtless one factor was that the deportees of the southern kingdom were allowed to remain together and to govern themselves in many matters, in contrast to the deportees of the northern kingdom in the eighth century, who had been broken up and scattered among the foreign populace.[14] Furthermore, the Judean leaders had had the benefit of almost two centuries more of prophetic teaching. In particular the great prophets Isaiah, Jeremiah, and Ezekiel had impressed themselves upon the consciousness of Judeans. They had not achieved much observable success with the people but indirectly and subconsciously they must have had a significant impact upon the people. And when the familiar structures of state and religion evaporated, the steadying prophetic words of judgment and hope rose to fill the vacuum and to support the people.[15]

It is a mistake to think that the survival of the Jews proves that they were the people of God. No external or disconnected facts can prove God's purpose and plan. There are some historical analogies to the persistence of a minority people in a similar manner, as, for example, the Armenians. Had the people disappeared with the nation, that would have been the end of the astonishing belief in the sole invisible God who wanted to reach the nations through a people. Instead of putting an end to this belief, the exile strengthened it. Numerically, it may be that a smaller number of Jews continued to hold to this belief but, qualitatively and creatively, those who did were vastly strengthened by the shock of the exile.

Among the most penetrating passages in the prophecies of Isaiah of the exile are the so-called Servant Songs.[16] Here is described the patient, persistent teaching function of God's Servant to the nations. In the first Servant Song (Isa. 42:1-4), God tells of the call and initiation of the Servant by the divine Spirit and of the Servant's teaching of justice to the nations. In the second Song (49:1-6), the Servant speaks of his preparation, despair, and final universal task. In the third Song (50:4-9), the Servant laments his outer persecution but finds consolation in his teachability and trust in God. In the final Song (52:13–53:12), God declares the vindication of his Servant, who is rejected and put to death, and the nations lament the Servant's suffering but confess that through him they have been brought near to God.

Who is this weak and struggling Servant who emerges ever and ever stronger, perfected and glorified in his weakness? If we listen to the text we are told that the Servant is the people of God, "My Servant are you, / Israel in whom I will be glorified." Israel is God's Servant. In his political death the nations are brought to God. He gives up life in order to grant life, dying he lives.

Yet the text also speaks at many points of the deafness and the blindness of the exiles and even of the task of the Servant in restoring Israel, "He who formed me from the womb as his servant, / to restore Jacob to him, / and to gather Israel for him." The Jews in exile both are and are not the Servant of God. They are no longer a political nation, but ethnically as well as religiously they are a people.

79

God's people is not simply to be equated with this Jewish community; God's people is called to life within this community. As in the preceding centuries, a prophetic minority was continually brought to life; so a minority in exile continues to bear the reality of God's purpose for all the rest. Wherever the faithful Jew responds, there the Servant Israel is at work.

A flood of imagery based on historical experience pours into the vortex of the Servant concept.[17] Moses as the patient lawgiver is there. David as the commander of nations is there. Jeremiah as the suffering prophet is there. Isaiah of the exile, with his own deeply personal apprehension of God, is there. Unnamed witnesses to God through all the centuries are there, and their number grows as the centuries unfold. Jesus Christ is there as the man of sorrows, as the Jew par excellence. And insofar as the people of God are alive and responsive in this hour, we or some of our contemporaries are there contributing details to the portraiture of the Servant.

It is not, however, an attractive portrait. It is marred by ugliness and matter-of-factness. It is not an "inspirational" painting; it is more like a Rouault than a Sallman. Those artists who really picture it are not the kind whose paintings we usually hang in our homes or churches. The Servant's beauty is the beauty of ugliness fully borne and transformed, but the ugliness remains as long as history remains, i.e., as long as God has a people to reach out to the nations.

What has the ugliness and desolation of the exile meant? It has meant retribution and punishment, but no theory of moral deserts can begin to explain it. It has meant a testing ground for faith. With the removal of external confidences, inner trust and discipline have been forged in the agony of the soul. Israel's history has come to this apparently sad and bitter end, decimation among the nations.

The Servant has labored through these centuries, prophets and priests have struggled, simple believers and trusting leaders have confessed their faith in word and deed. But it has led to meager results; it has ended on the dung heap of exile. "In vain have I labored, / for waste and void I have used up my energy." This waste and void is the *tôhû wābôhû*, "the waste and void" of Genesis 1:1. Chaos has returned; the promises of God to bring peace and fulfillment to human life have been frustrated and negated. The Servant has done all he could do and it has not been enough. But, like Job, he will not curse God and die. He merely waits on God, sitting without illusion in the presence of God, hoping for the second creation and the new exodus. There we too sit. "Therefore, my cause is with Yahweh, / and my reward with my God."

As the Servant pondered the import of his failure he heard a strange word from his God:

"It is too inconsequential [literally, "light a thing"] that
    you should be my servant /
  to raise up the tribes of Jacob, /
  to restore the surviving Israelites; //
So I will appoint you a light to the nations, /
  to be my salvation to the ends of the earth!"

The precious people of God is not precious enough to justify God's work with his Servant. The resounding declarations to Abraham, "In you all the earth's families will bless themselves" and to Moses and the people at the mount, "For I possess all the earth," echo through the bold assertion of God's intention for the Servant. History is much too important to God to limit his purpose to Israel. The Servant must help to restore the tribes in Palestine and to regroup the surviving exiles; but that is not enough. That is only the beginning. That is merely the first stage in the Servant's task to be "a light to the nations" and "to be my salvation to the ends of the earth."

While the Servant pouts and laments his condition, God calls him to a still larger responsibility. When Jeremiah had rebelled against his calling and accused God of hardness and deception, the only reply to the prophet was that he repent and strengthen himself for more work to do:

If you return, I will restore you, / before me you shall stand. //
If you declare what is precious, and not what is worthless, /
    you shall be as my mouth. //
They shall turn against you, / but you shall not accommodate
    to them. //
And I will make you to this people / a fortified bronze wall; //
They will fight against you, / but they shall not prevail over
    you, //
For I am with you / to save you and deliver you, // says Yahweh.
                                                    (Jeremiah 15: 19-20)

But what is there for the Servant to do beyond simply being God's people and waiting? How can God's people be "a light to the nations" and "a confederation for the nations" (Isa. 42:6) and "salvation to the ends of the earth" merely by doing nothing?

If it were not poetically dressed we might see at once how fantastic is the prophet's assumption. That this abandoned and powerless minority should do something for the nations is merely laughable. To hold such a worldwide mission before the fainting Servant is not to inspire but to mock him. God is once more playing his cruel jokes with men, putting impossible demands upon his people and then tantalizing them with dreams beyond fulfillment.

Indeed, if the nations find it incredible that in this weak people any real God could be found, so do the people themselves find it hard to believe. As the poet-prophet's rhetoric mounts, the spirit of the people flags. Through the nimbus of whipped-up enthusiasm, the stark flat facts protrude. This band of refugees holds onto the tatters of a religion, and this wild prophet consoles his people by telling them that they will bless the nations. Was ever opiate for a people more blatantly administered?

Or was it the authentic recollection of a people who knew itself to exist for the nations? Could it be that in its being sent from its home, it was being sent to the nations? Could this unwilling mission have been God's way of reaching the nations?

We wish that we knew how the Jews lived in their scattered condition, how they were organized and how they worshiped, with whom they had contacts and what they said to others about their religion. Here is at least one man from that time of forced detention who had come to believe that the Servant Israel had gone into exile in order to go to the nations and to lead them back with him to Palestine.

Should we call this a missionary faith, as it has often been decribed? [18] Active attempts at conversion are not noticeable in this prophecy, yet it is shot through with the belief that the new king of the Near East, who is to be Cyrus, the Persian, will make faith in Israel's God the imperial religion. This he will do by restoring the Jews to Palestine and rebuilding the temple as the imperial cult. But this he could do only because the Jews first were scattered in Babylon where Cyrus could meet them and come to know of their faith. When they were weakest they were strongest. And their strength would henceforth be in their quality of life and worship as the people of God, the priests of the nations.

There is a hidden paradoxical relation between surrender and glorification. The people who have not tried to make a name for themselves will become a name; those who do not want to be the center of the world will become its center. And they will find their glory in a perpetual self-giving, to teach the history and vitality of their God and to minister for the nations in constant sacrifice and song.

It is a vast and strange vision of the exile, compounded of lowly suffering and imperial triumph. God shall bring resolution to the conflict between his people and the nations by grafting the two together. The nations shall be brought into one great empire by Cyrus the Persian and all the nations shall consent to the common worship of Israel's God: one world; one faith; one priestly people!

But the prophet was wrong in his timing. Cyrus built an empire and restored the Jews to Palestine, but the nations did not convert to Yahweh, and Israel was not the priestly center for the nations. She remained in her divided state as a half-restored, half-scattered people. And so she still is and so the church still is, in spite of the efforts here and there to make Judaism or Christianity look like the official religion of a certain state or empire. The nations have not converted even when they have simulated the poses and trappings of the people of God. Church and culture are neither simply fused nor joined in a compatible alliance.

The veil remains over the nations. The light to the nations that went forth in Christ has not yet dispelled the darkness of the nations. Men wander back and forth between the darkness and the light, often in their double roles of worldling and believer, but the body of God's humanity has not yet been formed into one body. History moves on in its divided state. The Servant still suffers and hopes, fails and longs, is desolated and comforted. The nations still boast and pose, doing God's will and defying it, keeping his peace while defacing his earth and his image in man.

How long?

We do not know, for we have not been told.

What we do know is that we must go to the nations, to the world. We do know that in the hard facts of our life where we work and live, we are not merely forced and pushed from without but we are sent from within. We have gone to the nations and we are God's people there. The nations roar and rebel and weep in their frustration, but the people of God is always there in the form of its work as merchants and officials, scientists and technicians, farmers and factory workers.

Throughout we know that we have not been called for our own sakes. It is insufficient to love ourselves and what God has done for us; we are a bond of love to the nations. It is insufficient to praise this little circle of light; we are a light to the nations. Wherever we rest content within the fellowship of love, love is denied; wherever we trim the lamps, the flames gutter and go out.

But the worst part of it all is that we do not know how to reach the nations. We declare God's wonders but we have so little to offer. Our gestures are feeble and our example disgusting or pitiable. We do not want to commend ourselves although we do so ceaselessly. We proselyte too proudly and are humbled. Cyrus will not listen to us, and the nations are only mildly amused by us unless we happen to question their right to defame God's image by such profanities as racial discrimination and indiscriminate warfare.

It is a fearful thing to know that without you the nations

85

cannot be blessed and at the same time to be without a program that can offer a measure of hope. It must be that God will touch life with life and that one of the things we must keep surrendering to him is our illusion of mastery, our fascination with programs. The people of God go to the nations because they have been pushed and driven there in all their daily activities, out there into the world and down deep into the world that is within them. Once there they go about their work and they wait. In such profane and decidedly unglamorous ways the Servant will speak to the nations and then someday the veil that covers the nations will be taken away. God's people cannot themselves take it away, but without his people God tells us he cannot remove it.

Even so, it is not easy to wait alertly without deserting in impatience or falling asleep in apathy.

# D. CULTURE
# APPROXIMATES THE CHURCH

## *Isaiah 19:18-25* *

In that day there shall be five cities in the land of Egypt speaking the language of Canaan [i.e., Hebrew], and swearing by Yahweh of hosts. One of them shall be called the City of Righteousness [or "City of the Sun"].

In that day there shall be an altar to Yahweh in the midst of Egypt and a memorial pillar to Yahweh at its border, and it shall be a sign and witness to Yahweh of hosts in the land of Egypt; for they shall cry to Yahweh because of their oppressors and he shall send them a deliverer and he shall contend for and rescue them. And Yahweh shall make himself known to Egypt, and the Egyptians shall know Yahweh in that day and they shall present meat and cereal offerings and they shall vow vows to Yahweh and perform them. And Yahweh shall strike Egypt, striking and healing, and they shall return to Yahweh and he shall be receptive and heal them.

In that day there shall be a highway from Egypt to Assyria, and Assyria shall enter Egypt and Egypt shall enter Assyria and Egypt shall worship with Assyria.

In that day Israel shall be a third part with Egypt and Assyria, a blessing in the midst of the earth which Yahweh of hosts blessed, saying, "Blessed be my people Egypt, the work of my hands Assyria, and Israel my inheritance."

THIS concluding Old Testament passage on the people of God among the nations is by all odds the least familiar of

* Related passages: Isa. 1:26-28; Zeph. 3:9-10; Jer. 46:25-26; Ezek. 29:13-16; Isa. 45:14-17; Zech. 14:16-19; Mal. 1:11; Matt. 12:41-42; 25:31-46; Rev. 11:15-18.

the four we have studied. It is curious that this most universal Israelite prophecy should be so consistently neglected
by biblical exegetes.

Probably the four prophecies, each beginning with the
refrain "in that day," are not from the prophet Isaiah of
Jerusalem. On the other hand, nothing in the passage suggests that they were written as late as the exile and much
favors a time not later than the religious and social reformation of Josiah in 621 B.C.[19]

It cannot be known whether one or more persons are
responsible for the four prophecies. There is no simple or
obvious progression of thought from one to another, although as they now stand it is possible to trace a widening
perspective from one to the next. But there is no way of
knowing whether a single author or a collector of traditions
has arranged this order.

What we notice at once is that all the prophecies are
concerned with Egypt and the last two also include Assyria.
Together these nations were the two colossi of ancient Near
Eastern politics, between whom Israel was caught in the
juggernauts and squeeze plays of diplomacy and war. The
prophecies appear at the conclusion of a long condemnatory
prophecy against Egypt, and the change of mood grows as
we move toward the climax of the salvation of the nations
in a total religious unity.

The notion of an altar in Egypt where worship of God
could be conducted as well as at Jerusalem probably means
that the prophecy was written before Josiah made Jerusalem
the sole place where sacrifice could be offered to Israel's
God. The immediate stimulant for some or all of these pro-
Egyptian oracles may well have been increased contacts between Judeans and Egyptians. Long before the exile, Jews

were doubtless migrating to Egypt and, although we have little information, it is likely that Jewish military colonies were established in Egypt under Pharaoh Psamtik I (663-609), who depended greatly on foreign mercenaries to supply his army.[20]

The first prophecy tells of five cities that shall speak Hebrew, one of which is to be called, depending upon how one reads the text, either "City of Righteousness" or "City of the Sun." These may be five cities in which Jewish colonies were located, and thus would be the first cities to convert to worship to Yahweh. More likely, however, the five cities are merely symbolic of the five Amorite fortresses of Canaan which Joshua defeated when he conquered Canaan.[21] Those cities were the first fruits of Israel's taking of the land. Similarly, Israel will have five cities' worth of Egyptian converts before the total conversion occurs. This is an especially attractive interpretation if we take "City of Righteousness" as the original reading. In that case the meaning is that one of the five cities will be the Egyptian Jerusalem, the site of the central shrine, which Isaiah had called "the city of righteousness, the faithful city" (1:26).

The second prophecy tells of sacrifices and vows to Yahweh offered by the Egyptians in their own land. It is not necessary for them to come to Jerusalem. Palestine is no longer the religious center of the world in the same way that it was even for the earlier Isaiah and also for the later Isaiah of the exile.

God will send a "deliverer" to rescue the Egyptians from their oppressors. This is a good description of Psamtik I, who was the first of the Delta kings from Sais, a native ruler who threw off control of Egypt by the Assyrians. The latter under Essarhaddon and Ashurbanipal had invaded Egypt and administered severe blows to the land of the Nile. Now the land will be swept clear of Assyrians and the former "striking" of Egypt will be seen as "healing." Yahweh will be receptive to Egyptian prayers and he will heal the Egyptian people.

In this late pre-exilic prophecy's attitude toward Egypt we have come virtually full circle from the attitude predominating in the Exodus traditions. Yahweh, the smiter of Egypt, is at last the healer of Egypt. Adversity and defeat for Egypt are not terminal but instrumental to national solidarity and health. There is a startling and seemingly incongruous connection between God's destructive action among the nations and his constructive work among them. Just as the construction of Israel requires destructive chastening, so the initial destruction of the nations contributes to an emerging divine work of construction as God's chief goal for humanity.

The third prophecy envisions a great highway from Egypt to Assyria along which traffic will freely move from one land to the other. The road already existed but it had been as often the route of conquest and rapine as of trade and amity. Now the traditional enemies, Egypt and Assyria, the cold-war antagonists of the seventh century B.C., will freely intermingle. Above all, they will worship together. Presumably this means that worship of Yahweh will be as freely conducted in Assyria as in Egypt, for no land will be profane, unfit for him—no people unworthy of him. All will render their adoration and goods to Israel's God.

The last prophecy rises to unprecedented heights:

In that day Israel shall be a third part with Egypt and Assyria, a blessing in the midst of the earth which Yahweh of hosts blessed, saying, "Blessed be my people Egypt, the work of my hands Assyria, and Israel my inheritance."

The great political powers, Egypt and Assyria, and the religious leader, Israel, will be conjoined as the three parts of a confederation. Alone in the Old Testament a people other than Israel is called God's people, "my people Egypt." The full measure of God's solicitude for his people is no longer reserved for Israel; it is shared with other peoples. The nations participate in the blessing that God has intended for them from the beginning.

The truth of God's guidance of the nations had been stated openly by Amos:

"Are you not like the Ethiopians to me,
     O people of Israel?" says Yahweh.
"Did I not bring up Israel from the land of Egypt,
     and the Philistines from Caphtor and the Syrians from Kir?"
(Amos 9:7)

But while Amos had spoken those words in wrath and warning against the presumption of Israel to be God's favorite,[22] the prophet who speaks in Isaiah 19:25 does so without rancor and with steady eye foresees far more than the shadowy workings of God in the migrations of the nations; he sees, rather, their conscious and amicable participation in the worship of God and their full and free association one with another.

The straining of the people of God toward fulfillment in the nations has reached its outer limit. There is nothing that remains except for this people to cease to be peculiar. The special people no longer exists in the same way, inasmuch as all the nations are special. Israel has played her role and in God's plan has done her part.

But that is just the question: Will she now recede? In

fact, should the church simply wither away? Dare she so understand herself that she no longer cares for her own inner life except as it helps the nations to God? All the love and energy that have been lavished upon her devotion and service seem now to be cut short and forgotten. Surely God cannot overlook the long endeavor of his people and merely reward them as he rewards all the others. These other nations have certainly come so late to the vineyard that they cannot have the wages of God's people! Or can they? Isn't this what Israel wanted? Isn't this what the church cries out for night and day, the salvation of the nations? Or does it cry out more often for the "ecclesiasticizing" of the nations? Does it want the divine name glorified wherever the sun rises, or does it want its own name vindicated and celebrated? Does the church realistically know the difference between its own welfare as a self-contained institution and its welfare in the freedom of God?

Will the church really make room for the nations and take them as anything else but poor relations and second-class citizens of the kingdom, halfhearted laymen dependent on the priesthood of the church? A closely contemporary prophecy declares that after God has arisen as a witness and judge against the nations,

Yes, at that time I will change the speech of the peoples
   to a pure speech,
That all of them may call on the name of Yahweh
   and serve him with a single will [literally, "one shoulder"].
From beyond the rivers of Ethiopia
   the suppliants of the daughter of my scattered ones,
   shall bring me an offering.

(Zephaniah 3:9-10)

Here the center of the nations appears to remain parochially in Palestine, but the peoples are united in a single speech and a single will to worship God.[23]

The people of God has not been consistently gracious toward the nations that show signs of conversion. Israel did not noticeably open her heart to the nations. How does one open the heart toward those who are indifferent, oppressive, or contemptuous? The church does not welcome the nations in more than a subsidiary listening role. How can the closed guild of the churchly wise make room for the secular minds, systems, and skills that do not yield to theological formulas? They are of the profane world which must be baptized in the church's sanctity.

The people of God has come to a dead halt, staring at its own image, inwardly relieved that the response has not been too favorable from the nations, because to make room for the nations would mean to confess that God works not only through his people but beyond and in spite of them. In fact, the nations are to become his people. The special few who can explain themselves only if they are different must now be content with self-effacement and the extension of the fellowship of the redeemed beyond their previous comprehension.

"Israel shall be a third part with Egypt and Assyria." It is not easy to imagine Rome or Canterbury, or Constantinople, or for that matter any American denominational structure rejoicing that it is merely a third part with the United States and the Soviet Union or with Islam and Buddhism. If the veil were removed from the nations and we had no more materialists and atheists to flay, no more moral crusades to wage against gambling and communism, if we had to sit and listen and learn from the most profane of men—but the very thought is disgusting, and demeaning of God. That he does not ask of us.

Perhaps if all of us are so remade that we cannot recognize one another, such a universalism would be bearable, even delightful. If it is a fellowship of anything like the present run of men and nations, it is far safer to have an insulated church with its periodic review of virtues and ideals which can at least make life tolerable. But to risk God, to risk the possibility that God will reach the nations and forever render the people of God obsolete as we have always known it, is like asking a man to work himself out of his job. Do not ask of the church what is patently impossible!

Do we feel this way as churchmen because we have let our existence as the people of God become a separate status instead of a way of living in the world? Is it because we are so cut off from genuine involvement in our time and place that we cannot rejoice as members of the nations in the salvation of the nations? Are we mesmerized by churchly rite and jargon to the point that we cannot see that it is Assyria and Egypt who have been God's love all along, that it is real men and women, the real Israel, mankind typified in the church—not the papier-mâché religionists—whom he loves? It really would suit us if we could see ourselves as the people of God because we are, after all, somehow just a little bit better than the rest. But to be the people for no certain moral reason, just to serve as God's beachhead in this world without fanfare and subtle superiority feelings, is more than we want to bother with. To be no more exclusively serviceable to God in the end than Assyria and Egypt is difficult for Israel to accept. To be no more holy or necessary than

94

all other sorts of economic, social, and political bodies is bitter gall to church and synagogue.

Which is to say that the church more often falls back upon its traditional privilege than strains forward toward its consummation and demise.

# E. DYNAMICS OF THE ISRAELITE CHURCH-CULTURE IMAGES

## 1. The Images Summarized

*Exodus 19:2b-6:*
BELIEF in Israel's communion with God emerges solidly in connection with Moses and the exodus.

Israel is acutely aware that she is *a people in the midst of the nations and yet unlike the other nations,* is that she is "holy, a kingdom of priests." Israel's remarkable distinction is that God accompanies her in space and time. That must be maintained as the first great fact even if one eventually speaks of *the importance of individual belief* and of *all the nations as God's people.* Individualism and universalism are flowerings and not negations of particularism.

The God who so limits himself to Israel is the God of all men. God as Creator of all men is simultaneously the Redeemer of Israel. He is free to choose his course with deliberation. It appears that he wants this people for the sake of the world, for the benefit of all nations. *He will approach the nations not directly but mediately through Israel.* He will act through Israel not because of that people's particular fitness or virtue. Whenever Israel posits her peoplehood on some inner quality she cuts herself off from the God who chooses her and from the people who await her.

Perhaps the chief incongruity of the exodus events in the light of such a basic belief is the stark fact that God seems to be destroying the nations, or at any rate the Egyptians, instead of seeking their good. Can the smiter of the nations also be the healer of the nations?

The people in communion with God are a people in permanent and ordered communion. They are to be his people in the awesome context of obedience. The grace of God demands and entails the *if* of obedience but His grace also precedes and actualizes obedience. Every segment and role of life is the sphere for obedience, yet to sever obedience from grace is to consign them both to unreality. Only the presence of the gracious One can transform the *if* from threat to promise, from command to blessing, from death to life. The nation is holy not in its flawless performance but in its receptiveness and its direction.

*The primal biblical confidence that Israel has been chosen as a special people* perseveres through all the history of synagogue and church. It prevails in spite of the grossest abuse of the notion. It endures primarily not as a dogma but as an experience of God's free grace among men, which continually constitutes men in fellowship with him and their fellows. To be God's people in any age means to suffer a split between all the easy identities of the world—including the role of being "religious"—and the less secure identities of a people marked by a call and a hope. Only the whole of history can manifest that call and hope, reveal and vindicate them in their fullness. Yet the beginning of the experience of communion with God, as reported of Moses, shows that the experience has maintained a surprising continuity throughout Jewish and Christian history.

*Isaiah 2:1-4:*
*The people of God is always in transit. Its experience of God, its own culture and its task in culture always change*

*as its context changes.* Isaiah's world was that of Israel's emergence into the main flow of world history. Assyria confronted Israel as the most powerful and threatening force ever to appear in Palestine. Similarly, the nations come to the fore in eighth-century prophecy as in no previous period of Israelite history and in no earlier segment of Israelite literature.

Israel was faced with the theological meaning of her political and military struggle which had begun two centuries before under David. How was national security to be reconciled with faith in God? Israel vacillated, but Isaiah insisted on a taut connection between life's "necessities" and God's "realities."

Isaiah epitomizes the prophetic attack upon domestic injustice and upon belligerent and fear-ridden foreign policy. The essential sin of nations is a prideful overconfidence. Israel and Judah, on the one side, and Assyria and Egypt, on the other, will be judged. The prophet lived to see Israel overwhelmed, Judah reduced to an Assyrian satellite, and the Assyrian attack on Jerusalem frustrated. Yet these events did not seem to teach the participants anything; they did not visibly "repent," i.e., they did not change their proud and insecure views of themselves and others.

The problem is very clearly and sharply posed. *Israel must survive in order to be God's people but, having survived, she tends to lose her witness in emulation of national self-interest and fear.* We may readily see in this dilemma the dilemma of the church, accommodating to the world in order to command the attention of the world, but simultaneously ceasing to penetrate, to leaven, to summon, and to revolutionize.

Isaiah develops the theme of Jerusalem as the center of

98

the world, but in a novel way. Jerusalem is to hold its place by persuasion instead of by force. Not military coercion but the attraction of Israel's teaching about God is to win the consent of the nations. The voluntary gathering of the nations to Jerusalem will open a new era in human history, an era of peace and justice for all peoples.

A common belief in Israel's God will provide a frame of reference for settling disputes and the means for resolving differences between nations will be the instruction of Israel's God through the medium of the prophets.

Isaiah saw that only a community of consent could hold the nations in unity. Man has "learned" war; it is an apparent necessity only because socio-political habit has distorted man's vision. Man can "learn" peace when he wills, but to learn peace he must learn his own position in humility and confidence. Peace is based on self-understanding rooted in understanding of the Creator of nations and men.

Translated into history, *the learning of peace calls for a new center and focus for the nations.* The people of God must emerge not as the defenders of this or that nation-state but as the lodestone for the nations.

Isaiah 49:1-6:

When Judah joined Israel in exile, the hopes for reconstituting the nations around Jerusalem seemed dashed. The Jews had been dispersed, they had gone to the nations to be sure —but involuntarily. Isaiah of the exile sees a divine purpose in this dispersal just because he maintains an unbounded faith in the power and purpose of God in history and sees signs of God's current activity in world affairs.

Isaiah of the exile was insistent upon the continuity of God's purpose even though the people of God had ceased to live a normal life as an independent state. The possibilities for the future lay entirely with God and he could do new things with his people which they as yet could not imagine. Historically speaking, the fairly lenient policies of the Babylonians and the work of the prophets were factors in the survival of the Judeans in exile. Instead of putting an end to the experience of being God's people, the deportation and detention in Babylon intensified the experience of God for many Jews.

The Servant is no simple symbol; he is not merely the empirical Jewish community. *God's people are called to life and take shape within the empirical community.* Imagery drawn from many faithful Israelites has entered the composite portrait. Jesus Christ, as well as many faithful Jews and Christians, contributes to our contemporary reading of the Servant-symbol.

The attraction of the Servant is not in his symbolic beauty but in his devotion to life-oriented response to God and thereby to a transformation of ugliness into beauty, and in the rejoining of the fragmented lives of men and peoples.

The ugliness and desolation of exile are evident in the Servant-image. Israel's recent experience has been a time of testing and of waiting. It has been a time to discover the limits of human accomplishment—even the limits of religiously dedicated human effort. The Servant has done all that he could but it has not seemed to be sufficient. Many Jews give no attention to God's claim; most non-Jews take no interest in the Jewish report about God.

What is to come, therefore, must be the work of God: a second creation, a new exodus. The result will be a breaking out of the church into the world. Valuable as it is to God, *this people has its supreme value in that it is humanity in* embryo; *it is the nucleus of redeemed mankind.* Israel is valuable because God can see in her the value of all the peoples. And even more significantly, Israel will be the means by which God comes to the nations with his "light" and his "salvation."

How can Israel's going to the peoples be realistically conceived? What does Israel do besides wait for the nations to come to her? Her status was that of a displaced and powerless minority in a politically mature and culturally proud empire. Was such a summons the fantasy of a poetic mind or the calculated dogmatic justification for recent tragic events?

We wish that we knew more about the life of the Jews in Babylon and about the contacts of Isaiah of the exile with his own people and with non-Jews. Yet some things are reasonably clear from his writings. For one thing he insisted that a new power would shortly replace Babylon in Near Eastern affairs; Cyrus, the Persian, would be world ruler and he would make faith in Israel's God the imperial religion. He would be Constantine to ancient Judaism. A restored Jewish people would rebuild Jerusalem as the center of the imperial faith.

In this concept we note a paradoxical relation between the present lowly status of Israel in exile and the imminent glory of her role in the New Age. Lowly suffering and neglect are in contrast to imperial triumph and acclaim. Nonetheless, *the triumph and glory are of a peculiar kind, making no room for political or military dominance.* It is solely in the observance of her faith in God of the peoples that Israel will be honored.

*Isaiah 19:18-25:*

This most universal Israelite prophecy, consisting of four brief oracles, comes probably from a follower (or followers) of Isaiah in the seventh century, prior to Josiah's Reformation of 621 B.C., at a time when Jews were beginning to live in Egypt. All four oracles are about Egypt and the last two include Assyria, the two colossi of ancient Near Eastern politics. They are attached to a condemnation of Egypt and the shift to a motif of salvation becomes stronger as the oracles progress.

The first oracle (vs. 18) seems to picture the initial conversion of some Egyptian cities to Israel's God as a foretaste of later total conversion. These converts are likened to the five cities in Canaan that Joshua first conquered when he entered the land. One city will be the Egyptian Jerusalem.

The second oracle (vss. 19-22) declares that Egypt will worship in its purified land, swept clean of invaders by a "deliverer" (Pharaoh Psamtik I?). It will not be necessary for Egyptians to come to Palestine, since that land is no longer the religious center of the world. Yahweh, the smiter of Egypt is also the healer of Egypt.

The third oracle (vs. 23), using the image of the great Syro-Palestinian highway that bridges the two centers of power in the Near East, envisions free movement between Egypt and Assyria and the joint worship of Yahweh by both great peoples in both lands, since all lands and peoples are potentially holy, i.e., capable of being dedicated to and used by Israel's God.

The fourth oracle (vss. 24-25), pictures Egypt and Assyria and Israel in a three-part confederation conceived apparently on the analogy of the confederation of Israelite tribes. God can even say, "My people, Egypt."

This assertion goes beyond the claim of Amos that God controls the origins and current history of non-Jewish peoples to declare, without qualification, that *the nations will consciously and amicably participate in the worship of God while freely and fully associating with one another politically and culturally.*

This prophecy appears to have reached the outer limit of biblical thought about the relation of the people to the peoples, of church to culture. What it affirms is that the religious importance of the distinction between Israel and the nations is one day to be done away. A special people will no longer be needed because all people will have become special.

Israel will wither away as a theological necessity, but all that Israel stood for will be fulfilled among men as they learn to be true men.

Such passages as Isaiah 19:18-25 seem adamant in the rejection of a concept of progressive or gradual assimilation of the world's people to Israel. Israel shares with the nations, stands alongside them, apparently does not disappear, but also does not assimilate the other peoples. The peoples of the world confess Yahweh and worship him, but they do not become Israelites. *Israel remains as an ethnic and cultural phenomenon but she is no longer a theological* sine qua non.

## 2. Church-Culture Interaction-Patterns of Demarcation, Incorporation, Attraction, and Approximation

The four images of church-culture relations in ancient Israel, which we have examined against the backdrop of ancient Israelite thought about the people of God, exhibit certain persisting patterns.

Fundamentally the ancient Israelite tradition stresses a *distinction, even a tension or incongruity, between Israel as the people of God (church) and the surrounding structures and values (culture).* The uniqueness of the church is clear even in the broadly "universalistic" passages. The distinction cannot be reduced so as to produce a simple continuity or identity of church and culture. Nor can it be so heightened that the tension becomes entrenched opposition, or the distinction gives way to total separation.

*Of equal importance with the distinction of church against culture is the constant communication between church and culture,* the points and types of contact and conflict varying considerably from time to time. This is another way of saying that the church and the culture are themselves continuously evolving and are brought in touch with one another in endlessly changing patterns which are not easily predicted in advance.

An emphatic frontier exists between church and culture but it is a deceptively shifting boundary with strikingly varied activities occurring along and across it, ranging from friendly commerce to open hostility.

Nevertheless, *church-culture relations are not sheerly*

arbitrary or fortuitous. They display definite recurring patterns, rhythmic impulses, and metabolic processes.

The first pattern is the thrust toward *formation* and *demarcation* of the church. The pattern is strongest in the exodus-Sinai traditions but underlies all the images we have examined. Israel is shaped in covenant and sustained in communion as a sharply distinguished people. The movement of this pattern is inward toward a nucleus of faith and order. The mood is marked by adoration of God and concomitant preoccupation with his worship and service and with the proper shaping of the community.

This primal pattern is both the genius and the vulnerability of the church. When uncorrected by counterthrusts it veers toward lopsided narcissism and sheltered religiosity. It degenerates too often into worship of a safely aloof deity by a contentedly isolated sect.

Happily the people of God has repeatedly experienced powerful counterpatterns running against the tide of self-centeredness. The first of these rises within Israel as a drive for *outreach* and *incorporation* of culture, a drive that seeks communication with other peoples, an understanding of them, even a borrowing from their best features, and at times the impulse to draw them within the church. This thrust toward incorporation is not alone what has been characterized as proselyting or missionary work. It is an outward impulse aimed not exclusively at converting other people but directed as often at appreciating and drawing on their values and cultural forms. The movement is outward toward an expanding periphery. The mood is curiosity and exaltation at God's manifold creation. This impulse is well illustrated in Isaiah, chapter 49, and is at least in the background of Isaiah, chapters 2 and 19.

The stabilizing centrifugal force of expansion toward culture corrects the withdrawing centripetal impulse of the church cut off from culture. It adds relevance and zest to Israel's faith but may incline toward superficial syncretism or dilettantism, on the one side, or toward naïve missionary fanaticism, on the other.

The next two counterthrusts serving to balance the main thrust of the church in distinction from culture arise not from church but from culture. God's initiative in his world does not depend solely on the church. He works in other ways, for he is Lord of the culture as he is Lord of the church.

The first of the culture-originated forces is the impulse of the world to come to Israel, i.e., the *attraction* of culture to the church. The nations find an appeal in Israel's faith and life, and seek to learn of Israel or even to attach themselves directly to Israel. The movement is inward toward the church as an ordering nucleus for the confused multiplicity of the world's thoughts and deeds. The mood of Israel is receptivity toward the inquiring culture and her concern is to offer her life to God as the center for a new humanity. Isaiah, chapter 2, demonstrates this mood openly, and it is also evident in Isaiah, chapter 49, since it is obviously not inconsistent with the belief in Israel's attraction to the world.

The effect of this impulse from the world is to enhance belief in God as creator and to make tangible and believable Israel's frequently conventional dogma about the unity of the human race. Its danger is that it will be resisted as a threat to Israel's distinction or will be converted into a subjugation of the inquiring culture as a mere appendage of Israelite culture.

The final pattern of counterbalance is the *approximation*

of culture to the church in the sense that culture will carry out the functions and live by the values normally associated with the church. This means in effect that culture has become church in key respects. Without having to acknowledge the church or subject itself to churchly judgments, the culture becomes the bearer of God's grace—and not only his judgment. Culture comes into its own as "sacred" insofar as it reflects the gracious creative and preservative work of God. This view comes to expression in Isaiah, chapter 19, and also, in a measure, in the context of Isaiah, chapter 49, with its prophetic confidence in Persia as a kind of secular messianic power.

The basic movement conceived in this pattern is neither from church toward culture nor from culture toward church —although communication is open between them—but rather a parallel oscillatory movement by church and culture back and forth between the variously discerned actions or mandates of God and the men to be variously served by them. In our terms, allowance is made for religious and cultural pluralism. History's meaning cannot be subsumed simply under church or culture. Each reflects the will of God the Creator and Redeemer, and his will is to be done by the harmonious association—but not necessarily the outright confusion—of covenanted community and natural community. The tempers of church and of culture must be nondefensive and cooperative but not blandly syncretistic.

The contribution of this culture-based pattern is to chasten the urge to self-glorification and ecclesiastical imperialism in the church. Its weakness is to offer a tempting rationalization for churchly lethargy or for superficial syntheses that erode the distinction between church and culture so that church is not redemptive enough to save and culture is not natural enough to preserve.

For analytical purposes we have sought to "freeze" several moments in the ancient Israelite concept of church-culture relations, but it should by now be perfectly plain that the moments so discerned are understandable only as *structural elements, movements, or accents within a dynamic whole.* The images we have plumbed, as well as many others which could have been explored, tend to put their stress on one or the other of the leading elements. At the same time, additional elements tend to be present as presupposition or as accompanying nuance. *The total effect is of a pattern-complex—no single element being able to stand alone—within the church-culture continuum* (if similarity is stressed) *or the church-culture polar field* (if dissimilarity is stressed), involving at a minimum: *church-demarcation from culture, church-incorporation of culture, culture-attraction to church, and culture-approximation to church.*

# PART III

# CHURCH-CULTURE INTERACTION IN ANCIENT ISRAEL AND MODERN CHURCH

THE patterns of ancient Israelite church-culture interaction characterized in the preceding section according to their dominant aspects (demarcation, incorporation, attraction, approximation) are potentially important patterns in contemporary church-culture dynamics. But that may be no more in itself than to say that men have had essentially the same problems everywhere and at all times. We must now focus upon some of the urgent issues in current church-culture relations in order to see if any specific clues from the biblical-prophetic patterns will be of assistance in clarifying the issues and perhaps even in solving some of the more intractable problems in the relation of church and culture. Is there, in fact, some paradigmatic value to the ancient Israelite concept of "church" and its relation to culture patterns?

# A. ISRAEL AS
# "CHURCH"—CHURCH AS "ISRAEL"

THE place to begin our inquiry into the present is with a defense and amplification of the presupposition underlying this study, namely, that ancient Israel was a prototype of the modern church. Only if this thesis is tenable is there any likelihood that the Mosaic-prophetic faith will provide instructive insights for the present. Also, we must examine the implications of the continuity of Israelite, Jewish, and Christian belief for the present status of Judaism and the relation between church and synagogue. This subsection is, therefore, in part a probe into the legitimacy of a methodology of Christian ethics and theology that draws on Old Testament data centrally but selectively. In part, it is an exploration of Jewish-Christian ecumenics.

The continuity between ancient Israel and the modern church and synagogue as constellations of belief and practice is twofold: a continuing historical development and a persisting spiritual type. The emergence of Jews and Christians in recent centuries out of the Israelite past is absolutely clear in principle even when details of the process are obscure. We know, for example, that the synagogue as a religio-cultural institution developed out of the conditions of Israelite exile and that the church as a religio-cultural institution was in turn patterned upon the synagogue, although ample room for debate and conjecture remains as to precisely when and how the respective developments occurred and were related.[1]

That the Jewish synagogue is a decisive outgrowth of ancient Israel is less debatable than that the Christian church is also such a decisive outgrowth. Yet the combination of ancient Israelite writings in Hebrew with the early Christian writings in Greek (to form Old Testament and New Testament) aptly symbolizes the unshakable consciousness of historical and spiritual continuity between Moses and the prophets, on the one side, and Jesus and his disciples, on the other, to which the Christians witnessed.

Yet it is equally true that the mere determination of historical dependence and development would not give modern significance to the earlier history. The chronological and developmental sequence must be shown in some way to possess fundamental cohesion and not simply temporal succession. Did Israelites have a revealing and ordering experience of God and of human life that is like later and contemporary Jewish and Christian experiences in important respects? It is one thing to show that Jews and Christians in earlier times affirmed their community with ancient Israel; it is yet another matter—and the one crucial for us— whether Jewish and Christian bodies still see this community as true in an operational sense in contrast to a merely traditional assertion.

The persisting spiritual type which binds Israelite, Jew, and Christian is the awareness of *historical communion with God*.[2] In all these admittedly very diverse bodies there has been and still is a prevailing sense of communion with God experienced in a community of men with historical boundaries. These are men with historic beginnings and historic destinies, as well as contemporary joys and duties. They are men in time but not wholly of time for they know of the Lord of Time.

The persistence of this spiritual type is more important than all the admitted differences between, among, and within Hebraism, Judaism, and Christianity. Efforts to show Judaism and Christianity as two different spiritual types, the former positive, practical and world-affirming and the latter negative, metaphysical and world-denying (generally the Jewish polemic) [3] or the former rigid, wrathful, and repressively legalistic and the latter flexible, grace-conscious, and love-centered (generally the Christian polemic) [4] are historically and spiritually mistaken. In fact, prophetic world-affirmation and apocalyptic world-denial, religious practice and metaphysics, conviction and adaptability, law and grace, wrath and love have struggled and merged in countless ways both in Judaism and in Christianity—precisely because all these elements have their roots in ancient Israel. It seems that the one objective way to describe the Jew is not to say that he is "positive," "world-affirming," "legalistic," "wrath-conscious," "a fossil," etc., but to say that he is the man who sees the historical communion with God focused in the line from Moses to the Talmud. And the one way to describe the Christian is not to say that he is "negative," "metaphysical," "world-denying," "progressive," "grace-conscious," "love-centered," etc., but to say that he is the man who sees the historical communion with God focused in the line from Moses to Jesus.

That Jews and Christians, in common with their Israelite progenitors, have thought and continue to think in terms of historical, communal, and traditional forms and truths focused moment by moment on direct personal encounter with God means that we are dealing with more than rhetoric when we describe the ancient Israelite community as "church" or when we call the church "Israel." We are able to do this in entire cognizance of historical variety in the various confessions and without any need to import explicitly Christian elements into Israel or to deny important analogues in the Israelite, Jewish, and Christian experiences and beliefs when they are patent. Not much historical or theological light will be thrown either way by Christians who dismiss a given view as too Jewish or by Jews who discount a position as too Christian. Ancient Israel was not as uniformly "Jewish" or "Christian" as we would sometimes have it; nor are Judaism and Christianity as monolithically "Jewish" and "Christian" respectively as their members sometimes believe. In such instances "Jewish" and "Christian" often describe cultural folkways instead of theological substance.

As one way of approach to the present relation of Jew and Christian theologically viewed, let us consider the early Christian conceptions of Jesus as Messiah, noting how these compared with current Jewish messianic views. Perhaps we can then have some basis for viewing the chief explicit theological basis for division between Jews and Christians: the difference in attitude toward Jesus of Nazareth and, collaterally, toward the manner in which the historical communion of God and man would be consummated.

The belief in Jesus as Messiah or Christ is understandable only in the light of a distinction between the broad Jewish hope in a redemptive future, i.e., eschatology in the wide sense, and belief in an individual Messiah, which was one but not the exclusive form of future hope.[5] Early Christianity was both eschatological and Messianic, but with two important caveats.

First, the Messianic model figure was reinterpreted so as to combine several of the eschatological redemption figures of the Hebrew Bible. The narrow sense of Messiah as a royal figure, as son of David, was not at all strictly adhered to—in spite of efforts in the New Testament to demonstrate the Davidic lineage of Jesus or to show that his birthplace was the Davidic Bethlehem. Along the lines of intertestamental writings such as Enoch, the New Testament tended, rather, to bring together originally separate models—the Davidic Messiah, the Suffering Servant, and the Son of Man —into one portraiture as the necessary way of expressing the decisive work of Jesus of Nazareth. The content of Jesus' own "messianic consciousness" has been intensively probed with largely inconclusive results.[6] We may, however, probably conclude that he himself preferred the title "Son of Man" (in the Danielic-Enochian sense) and that he thought of his words and deeds as vitally bound up with the immanent and imminent New Age.

Second, the functions of Messiah as God's agent in the redemption of the world were divided between the earthly life of Jesus of Nazareth and his expected return to this world in power. The teaching and suffering aspects of his first advent correspond best to the Suffering Servant and humiliated Son of Man models, whereas the cosmic judicial aspects of his second advent best accord with the traditional Davidic Messiah model. When Jews say that Jesus could not be Messiah because he did not bring the worldwide reign of peace and righteousness which the Messiah is to bring, they express precisely the understanding of the first Jewish Chris-

115

tians. They also fully understood that what Jesus had begun was an as yet unfinished revolution. As he had overturned their lives, he would one day overturn history. He was still Messiah incognito; although wonderfully vindicated by the Resurrection, Jesus appeared only to those close to him and not in an epiphany to overwhelm the world as he one day will.

The conclusion of such an understanding of the interrelation of Jewish and Christian Messianic beliefs is inescapable. The Messiah model was not so clearly delineated that Jesus or the early Church could tailor his life to fit a single traditional pattern. The role was richly varied and the related models of Suffering Servant and Son of Man were at hand to further enrich it or to stand in tension with it. Furthermore, Jesus was a novel individual who was not merely acting out some learned parts. He did what he understood God's will to be, partly in dependence on traditional models but partly under the impact of the Spirit, and afterward he had to be explained as best his followers could in the light of what he had said and done and with the help of the Hebrew Bible.

To put the theological issue sharply: What was at stake in the messianic discussions between Judaism and Christianity? Which religion offers the "true" interpretation of the Messiah?

To the first question we can now answer that at issue were various ways of understanding both the already experienced and the yet expected historical redemption of God. For both religions this redemption was understood as partially realized and yet to be consummated. For both, the redemption was experienced by a community of believing persons who formed the prototype of the future human community.

116

At variance was their understanding of the relevance of the work of Jesus of Nazareth as God's agent in his work of redemption. Closely associated was a variance in attitude toward the relative weight to be given to ceremonial law and to spiritual freedom.

To the question of validity of understanding, no answer from the historical sphere is possible. Certainly a great deal is gained by Christians and Jews when they try as objectively as possible really to see what has happened in their past and thus to dispel prejudices and misunderstandings. Nevertheless, there were and there are different value judgments involved. They are not as different, as irreconcilable, or as pompously literal as such religious judgments have often seemed. But they are at least real facts of spiritual and communal life. They cannot honestly be resolved by historical research or theological game-playing.

It is hardly realistic to suppose that Jews will readily become Christians when they can be shown that Jesus did actually fill some traditional category of Messiah or at least that he was not "un-Jewish." Nor will Christians become Jews when they discover that early Christian creedal formulations overlaid the Jewish elements in primitive Christianity with Greek philosophy. We have noted in earlier sections an Israelite fondness for the principle of *mediation*, whereby individuals were able to represent the group, to intercede for it, and to bring it spiritual benefits. That is perhaps the heart of what the modern Christian wants to say about Jesus. God's goodness is mediated to man through this representative man, without prejudice to the singleness of God's being and will. The meaning of history, true manhood, is best discerned in this Jesus. But that confidence at its core depends upon a personal evaluation that cannot be

117

made any the less necessary by centuries of Christian tradition. It is born of self-illumination, although greatly enriched and corroborated by other witnesses of past and present.

My point is simply this: Christians and Jews will have to talk about their beliefs at the deepest level of feeling where they drop out of sight in the unconscious and at their highest reaches where they lift the isolated self into the company of men and God. Study of religious history, for all its value, cannot bear the weight of religious experience. In such discussions a great deal is negotiable and discardable. Attitudes and defenses once thought to be the necessary weapons and stances of interfaith disputations are totally outmoded. We can well do without them, but we cannot do without that integrity for Christian and for Jew which simply will not be hoodwinked by verbal tricks and leveling formulas of compromise, which do not touch us religiously at the depths and at the heights.

Even so, although our rational minds and our theological systems cannot effect a resolution—and fortunately so, we should add!—historic change may establish new ground between the two religions. The messianic hope in its strict sense will one day cease to be the issue between Christians and Jews that it now appears to be. For what, after all, is the real issue concealed within the question of the Messiah? Is it not the question of how God shows his favor and redemption to man, how he shapes our human history to his ends? The symbols of Christianity and Judaism show a *basic type* but nevertheless form *two related and autonomous*, rather than identical or interchangeable, *sets of answers or clues to* how God works. Startling developments in man's understanding of his world and of himself are bringing rapid

118

changes in the interpretation of those symbols. We may be nearing the time when ardent devotion to one set of religious symbols will not seem to require rejection of all other sets of symbols. This need not entail religious indifference or dilettante syncretism. It could lead to a closer association between Christians and Jews resulting from awakening realization of their historic interconnections and their similarity in spiritual type. This closer association may assume presently unimagined forms.

One result of the historical examination of the religions of ancient Israel and of subsequent Judaism and Christianity should be a more realistic description of the latter as "sister" religions rather than as "mother-daughter" religions.[7] In one sense, of course, Christianity arose within Judaism and departed from it, and only on such a model can many elements of early Christianity and of Judaism itself be interpreted. But in a broader and theologically more significant sense, Judaism and Christianity arose concurrently and achieved their distinctive forms in considerable measure as a result of the varying ways they drew upon their common ancestral faith and reacted to one another.

Another way to state the relation between these "sister" faiths is to observe that in the first century of our era the legacy of ancient Israel was being built upon in manifold ways by Jewish groups contending for adherents. Eventually two of these became dominant—Pharisaic or Rabbinic Judaism and universalistic Christianity—and their views became largely determinative for what we know as Judaism and Christianity. Yet it must not be forgotten that many Jewish and Christian viewpoints were active at that time and still continue in fact in modified forms alongside of the dominant types. There are fundamentalists and progressives among Jews and Christians. There are Jews who want a larger place for Jesus of Nazareth than their religion has accorded him traditionally. There are Christians who desire a more dynamic symbolic interpretation of the person of Jesus than the formal doctrines of the Trinity and the Incarnation seem to have encouraged.

The superiority feelings and defensiveness of Jews and Christians will give way to the recognition that they are incomplete without one another.[8] Christianity is not to be dismissed as an aberrant offspring of Judaism, a second-best version of Judaism for Gentiles. Judaism is not to be scorned as a senile parent who refuses to give way to its enlightened progeny, a stubborn "fossil."

Judaism and Christianity are co-heirs of one historical type of faith as symbolized by the fact that they are cointerpreters of one Hebrew Bible. That each exists as a living confessional phenomenon is not an occasion for embarrassment to the other but a clue or sign of God's purpose that they must attempt to read constructively. Judaism can never be self-contained because Christianity has sprung from it and coexists with it. Christianity can never be self-contained because the Judaism from which it sprang has continued as a living independent force.

The coexistence of Judaism and Christianity has heretofore characteristically either been denied as an impossibility (requiring conversion or destruction of the other) or been conceded as an annoying necessity (official toleration accompanied by indifference or disguised hostility) or recognized as a historical fact or a socio-political necessity (inducing objective study in a pluralistic society where brotherhood is at a premium). Only sporadically and never officially have the respective existences of Judaism and

Christianity been incorporated by either religion into the very substance of the theological truth it wishes to assert. Each has wished to live as though the other is only a historical but not a theological reality.

So Jews and Christians in full mutual respect must study the Bible together and talk to one another about their inmost beliefs and uncertainties. They will continue at the same time to deepen their association in joint social and political study and action, but this public activity will be joined with study and conversation about what it means to be a Jew or a Christian. The interplay of action and theological reflection will shift the present polite but largely sterile coexistence into a frank and searching coexamination which cannot but lead in turn to copenetration in as yet unknown ways. Increasingly Jewish-Christian ecumenics will follow the course of Protestant-Catholic ecumenics.

What might such an alignment of action and conversation between Jew and Christian produce in the furtherance of church-culture and synagogue-culture relations? At the beginning it would be likely that adherents of each religion would show sharp awareness of the way culture had been accommodated by its opposite number. Christians would point out how Judaism's isolation from the dominant culture for many centuries had conditioned its belief and temper: its need for visible demarcating institutions and practices, its defensiveness and insularity, its sobriety and pessimism. Jews would as quickly witness to Christianity's acculturation to the prevailing Western civilization which affected it profoundly by stimulating fascination with philosophical and theological formulas and creedalism, use of the state's power to coerce in religious matters, acquiescence in social and political injustice. Behind these admonitions would lurk a decided bias to dismiss alien beliefs and institutions so saturated with cultural conformity or cultural reaction. But these open protests, these sincerely vehement accusations, would clear the theological air.

In a second stage of conversation, Jew and Christian would be respectively drawn toward a reckoning with the word of the other, no longer heard as accusation but, rather, as stimulant and witness. After all due allowance for defensiveness, misinformation, and caricature, the analysis by the opposite religionist would have to be grappled with as witness to the truth and as stimulant to new options in the present encounter with culture. The conversation would shift from the levels of historical report and of open or veiled accusation to the levels of self-analysis and of coinquiry, coinstruction and coaction. Jews and Christians who could really bear to maintain such an encounter in a continuing theological framework would discover that the new relation in which they stood to one another had itself become a novel form of confrontation with culture. The Jew would face at first hand the covenantal and cultural world of the Christian. The Christian would face at first hand the covenantal and cultural world of the Jew.

The prophetic principle in ancient Israel, namely, the power of the covenant faith to bring sustained constructive criticism to bear on the covenant community, would live again in a Judaism and in a Christianity which had set out to discover one another. The result, it may be predicted, would be, first, to reveal the culture struggles of the other faith for the first time as theologically significant and, second, to open up as yet unconceived pathways for both church and synagogue to fulfill their missions as the people of God in present culture.

The result of this inquiry has been to show that the Christian church may honestly recognize its prototype in ancient Israel and conceive of itself as a new kind of Israel. At the same time, somewhat surprisingly, it has been discovered that this two-way appropriation of insights between ancient Israel and modern church does not exclude the same appropriation between ancient Israel and Judaism. The viability and relevance of Judaism in the present is not ruled out or prejudged by the process. Contrary to much traditional Christian thought, the price of affirming the continuity of Israel and church is not the denigration of Judaism. Contrary to much traditional Jewish thought, the price of affirming the continuity of Israel and the synagogue is not the denigration of Christianity. Rather, that which clarifies and strengthens the church clarifies and strengthens the synagogue and equally that which clarifies and strengthens the synagogue clarifies and strengthens the church.

## B. THE CHURCH AND
## NONHISTORICAL RELIGIONS

WE have contended that Judaism and Christianity are
species of the historical genus of religion which sprang up in
ancient Israel. It is their common historical bent, and specifically a shared history and literature, which makes them
sister faiths and which forms the basis for an urgent ecumenical task of mutual discovery in order to fulfill their own
respective missions.

For the most part, the same line of argument will not
apply, however, when we turn to the other religions of the
world for they do not all have a covenantal core-faith. It is
true that Islam might be regarded as a third specimen of
historical religion since it shows dependence upon and similarity to Judaism in certain respects, notably its passionate
monotheism and its devotion to a book. But even if the
genus of historical religion were enlarged to include Islam,
and possibly Zoroastrianism because of its eschatology, it
would not be possible to argue in the same fashion for many,
if in fact any, of the other religions.

In any case we are forced to recognize that several of the
higher religions of the world are of another type than Judaism and Christianity. In them revelation of the divine and
the ordering of the good life are in some way regarded as
unaffected by history, or at the least they are not thought

of as fundamentally bound up with history, i.e., they are not communicated through a historical relation between God or the divine and the human community. These religions, in other words, are nonhistorical or, more precisely, noncovenantal. Such would be true of Confucianism, Shinto, Hinduism, and Buddhism.

One rather frequent way to give credence to the nonhistorical religions in Jewish-Christian terms has been to emphasize certain similarities between these faiths and Judaism or Christianity and then to elevate the supposed Jewish or Christian analogues in those religions to a central importance. It may be noted, for example, that Mahayana or northern Buddhism displays analogues to Christian concepts of salvation and sacrificial love. But this course is futile because it does not respect the integrity of the alien religion. Many of the analogous elements appear in constellation with nonanalogous features and the total meaning in context may not offer a particularly close parallel after all. The imperialistic pretension of the historical religion becomes clear since the nonhistorical religion is judged solely by how much it corresponds to or departs from Judaism and Christianity. Both the paucity of convincing parallels and the too provincial criteria for judgment make poor bases for viewing the relation between the historical and the nonhistorical religions.

Another course is simply to abandon a firm standing point in any of the religions, historical or nonhistorical. In this case an effort may be made to locate a common core in several of the religions and to piece together compatible or reasonably harmonious beliefs and practices drawn from many religious sources. This openly syncretistic approach is not without interest and even, in some cases, valuable results for the study of religion. As living religions, however, syncretistic constructs have not been effective to date. Sincere endeavors to bring elements of several religions together in one religion, as for instance in the Bahai sect, have not seemed spiritually authentic or attractive to followers of the bowdlerized religions. The chief reason seems to be the lack of a common historical experience to precipitate genuine communion and organic development. At some future date the religions of the world may grow together, but they cannot simply be put together as an exercise in logic or good will.

Of course the most common approach to the nonhistorical religions by Jews and Christians has been the overt missionary approach: to seek the conversion of their adherents. This position assumes the Confucian or Buddhist to be in error and in need of salvation. In principle this approach applies equally to Jew and Christian, although in practice Jews have had little opportunity since biblical times to proselyte and, owing to painful experiences of Christian pressure and coercion upon them, they have been hesitant to seek converts where they might have done so with impunity. Nonetheless, from time to time serious proposals are made within Judaism that it once again actively seek converts.

Yet in this century, just as Christian missions seemed to be making considerable strides, grave doubts have been cast upon the feasibility and the legitimacy of the approach. Many of the doubts arise from objective historical circumstances. The most fertile mission fields, once colonial wards of Christian powers, now lie in newly independent nations. The previously often moribund nonhistorical religions of those lands have frequently experienced renewal and revival.

In instances, as with Islam, countermissionary movements to roll back Christian gains have developed. Over all, the historical understanding of human nature, including man's religions, has undercut the absolute claims of the historical religions.

But a large part of the doubt about missions in the usual mold has come from the Christian fold itself, and not merely from ecclesiastical realists who insist on accepting the changed objective situation or from halfhearted or nominal Christians who know little about missions and are prepared to believe the worst. Second thoughts about missions have appeared among precisely those committed Christians who in other times would have been their most ardent champions. Many convinced Christians no longer believe in the attempt to convert adherents of other religions. They may try to soften or blunt this conclusion but it is often deeply rooted in a theological outlook. It cannot be dismissed as wishy-washy or bland toleration. It does not come from the belief that the religions of the world are simply all alike anyway. It does not blink at the fact that many crudities and horrors and outright untruths are to be found in these alien religions.

What is the theological basis of the new attitude toward the nonhistorical religions? To find the answer we must go back to the historical faith of ancient Israel. We discovered that at its very foundation the Israelite faith had a clear double aspect (see pp. 56-63). Primary to all else in it was the reality of covenant which was not, however, experienced in arbitrary isolation; of equal importance was the presupposition that the covenanting God was God of the world and of all history. The covenant faith was set in a creation faith. "You shall be my prized possession" was emphatically linked with and conditioned by "for I possess all the earth."

In the prophetic passages already examined the same conjunction of special history and general history, redemption and creation, is dominant. In prophecy, however, the direction of vision was turned more toward the present and the future than the past. As Yahweh had once selected a people from among all the peoples, he is now at work to reunite the separated peoples. His work with Israel has never led him to forget the other peoples. Israel has sprung from one world, lives in one world, will return to one world.

Granted this ecumenical vision of ancient Israel, was it not always assumed that the religion of Israel would replace the other religions? Would not Baalism and all the idolatries of Egypt, Assyria, Babylon, and Persia give way to worship of Yahweh? Did not the reunion of the peoples mean precisely the conversion of all non-Israelites to the faith of Israel? Does not the peculiar combination of covenant faith and creation faith in ancient Israel support the traditional Jewish and Christian views of a mission to convert men from all other religions to the one true religion?

The assumption that Israel's religion will replace the other religions is certainly very strong in the prophetic visions of the future. More accurately, it should be said that the common traditional Israelite assumption in this regard was reflected in the imagery and terminology of the prophets. But in this writer's opinion it would be wrong to regard the displacement of other religions by Israelite religion as a prescriptive dogma on anything like the same level as the covenant faith proper.

When examined carefully the three poetic eschatological passages in Isaiah indicate considerable ambiguity and variety of nuance on the question: What happens to non-Is-

128

raelite religions when God reunites the peoples of the earth? Isaiah, chapter 2, suggests that the reunion is a practical plan for resolving political tensions and that the chief role of Israelite religion will be in political mediation (see pp. 64-75). Isaiah, chapter 49, given its full context, foresees the reconstruction of an Israelite religious community in Palestine and the end of idol worship by Gentiles, but it does not foreclose nonidolatrous Gentile religious forms and practices (see pp. 76-86). (It has even been suggested that the prophet was aware of Cyrus as a Mithraist and Zoro-astrian and thus formally not an idolater, but the text is not explicit and it would be wrong to build an argument on the hypothesis.) In Isaiah, chapter 19, Assyria and Egypt worship Yahweh, but they do not have to do so in Palestine and apparently will be able to develop their own forms and institutions based on their own national experiences; they do not simply take Israelite religion on its own (see pp. 87-95).

Under the extreme pressures of the pre-exilic fight with Baalism and the postexilic struggle for Jewish survival, it was natural to emphasize again and again that all religions were a threat to Israel's faith. They were to be resisted as far as Israel was concerned; they must not seduce Israel into abandonment of her covenant faith.

But the creation faith of Israel that encompassed and embraced the covenant faith could not surrender the reality of God's indirect or veiled presence among all peoples. At the very least, they could be admitted to his worship in the community of Israel. At the most, some as yet unimaginable act of God would bring them into direct communication with Israel's God without the nations necessarily assuming Israel's religion as it had been previously known.

129

It was possible to take with complete seriousness the religious quest and thrust of non-Israelite peoples. Misguided as they might be from the point of view of covenant faith, dangerous as were their blandishments to the vigor of covenant faith, these peoples were Yahweh's creation and they reached after him as best they could. Yahweh's means for reaching out to all his peoples were not restricted to what Israel could do. Yahweh had a purpose for these peoples that Israel did not fully know and he had a strategy for incorporating them in his loving purpose which he did not divulge to his covenant people except in symbolic visions and apprehensions.

Judaism and Christianity took over from ancient Israel this double heritage in its attitude toward other religions: a predominant animus and distrust, on the one side, and a secondary but also unmistakable respect for the access to God which was available even through these nonhistorical religions. For Judaism this was expressed in the Noachian covenant which symbolized the direct relation of Israel's God with men everywhere apart from Mosaic law and prophecy.[9] For Christianity this was expressed by Christ as the pre-existent One, the Logos, who in his work as creator and provider gave light to men wherever there was light and who dealt through human conscience with every man even though he might be unfamiliar with Moses or Jesus.[10]

It is precisely this secondary, frequently neglected, but totally authentic traditional view toward nonhistorical religious experience which can give Jews and Christians courage for encounter with contemporary religions.[11] To be sure, it would be a grievous distortion of the old Israelite-Jewish-Christian pattern if the creation faith were sundered from the covenant faith. The irrefragable union of the two would

130

seem to preclude all possibility for using the creation faith as a justification for the sorts of superficial parallel-hunting and syncretistic patchwork which have so often discredited the whole endeavor to take man's quest for God in the other religions seriously.

Is there another alternative?

It may well be that the ecumenical awakening among Protestants and Catholics, as also the first stirrings of ecumenism among Jews and Christians, will give us the clue. Joint caring for and involvement in the issues of our world—united with serious conversation on the meaning of being Jew, Christian, Confucian, Hindu, Buddhist—would accord fully with the vital covenant and creation faith of the historical religions. For example, as Christians, Jews, and Buddhists in particular seek to deal constructively with revolutionary chaos in Southeast Asia they may find the basis for ecumenical encounter.[12] Instead of programmatic conferences or parliaments of religion, with exclusively theological agendas, the joint facing of live problems may be the one way open for men of such differing faiths to know one another not merely as believing abstractions but as historically involved believers.[13]

Yet another possibility for certain individuals may prove to be membership simultaneously in more than one of the religions. This could never be a general formula, but selected persons who have come to know two religions intimately might attempt to live inside both of them. It is interesting to hear the witness of a small number of Israelis who regard themselves as Jews and Christians, although their formal participation in Judaism and Christianity is less than satisfactory to either official communion.[14] Similarly, it might not be incompatible for the same person to be both a Christian and a Hindu. Conflicts over doctrine and practice and, perhaps more critically, over self-identity would be inevitable.[15] Such a person might be denied membership or be restricted or expelled from standing bodies of believers. He might even be required to settle in some cases for the role of "God-fearer," an inquirer living closely with but not fully joined to the faith. But such a mission, if genuinely integrated with one's life and not pursued merely as a gimmick, might build bridges of far greater permanence than the intellectualistic structures of syncretism.[16]

So we have ventured to see a possible progression leading from the now well-launched ecumenical venture of Protestant and Catholic, to a barely dawning ecumenical awakening of Jew and Christian, and lastly to an as yet scarcely conceived ecumenical encounter of the world religions. To many Jews and Christians this may sound distressingly like the long-discredited counsels of religious liberalism. On certain points there is undoubted affinity. Let us never forget, however, that things favored by liberalism, like those advanced by communism, are not automatically wrong. Just because history is novel, we may have better grounds and clearer guides in doing today what in other times might have been premature or poorly grounded.

Above all, however, the motive and spirit of Jewish and Christian participation in the ecumenical quest of the world's religions would be drawn from the font of ancient tradition, and it would move steadily on the ground of covenant and creation. It would be indebted to all historical and humanistic and technological insight but it would be soundly theological in its own right.

There is both an institutional and a faith risk in believing that God as known in Christ, or God as known in Torah, is the God known in other religions without insisting on the importation of Jesus or the Torah. There are far greater risks, however, in marking time in our proprietor role as the custodians of salvation for everyone. It is God of the covenant who creates and redeems men. The covenant forms do not create or redeem. We may be at the threshhold of a new exodus, when God is about to do "a new thing," which will appear initially as strange but will prove, in the long run, to be as liberating as the juxtaposition of religions and cultures in the Near East following the exile.

# C. THE CHURCH
# AND THE NATIONS

In order to put the present situation in context we shall briefly survey the major historical attitudes of Israel, synagogue, and church toward the state.

For many centuries biblical thought did not distinguish sharply between church and nation. To belong to the people of God was also to belong to the tribal league or to the kingdom of David or to the divided monarchies of Israel and Judah. When Israel and Judah lost political independence, a definite distinction arose between being a Jew and belonging to a particular political order. One could be a Jew in Palestine or in Egypt or in Babylon—in virtually any political arrangement—provided that one's religion could be practiced without serious disability. Yet the understanding that Jewish faith had political dimensions and implications was vigorously maintained by belief in the Messiah, who would restore righteousness and peace in the historical-political sphere and, as sometimes conceived, would even create a world wide Jewish hegemony over the nations.

Scrutiny of the church-culture patterns in prophetic thought shows that as early as Isaiah of Jerusalem a split began to develop between Israel's religious identity and its political identity. In treating of a faithful "remnant," Isaiah presupposed that not everything done by or in the Hebrew

134

state spoke for or accorded with the religious meaning and vocation of Israel. This belief was intensified in the later prophets. Although being a Jew never ceased to have collective ethnic significance, it did increasingly become dissociated from particular political orders and government policies.

Tension and conflict developed between the Jews as church and the various secular powers over them, Jewish and non-Jewish. A crisis was reached when the Hellenistic empire based in Syria (the Seleucids under Antiochus Epiphanes) tried to stamp out Judaism in the second century B.C. Similar friction arose sporadically under Roman emperors, although in general Rome granted political immunities to Judaism whenever religion was involved (e.g., an exemption of Jews from official emperor worship and from military service because of their refusal to fight on Sabbath). Occasional difficulties with Muslim states and more frequent ones with Christian states have marked the later course of Judaism. The "ghetto" was a political enforcement of a religious, social, and economic separate-but-unequal status on a recalcitrant minority.[17] Only since 1948, in Israel, has Judaism become again the religion of a state, as formerly in biblical times. Now, however, the aim of Israel to be both a theocracy and a democracy has led to problems in granting civic identity and full freedom to its Muslim and Christian minorities.[18]

Christianity has been marked by several phases in its church-state involvements.[19] It began as did Judaism with a mixture of attitudes toward the Roman political order whose religious grounds were in paganism, ranging from a mild appreciation for the order and protection it afforded, through indifference and neutrality, to tension and outright condemnation for the state's interference with and persecution of religious dissenters. When the late Roman empire, and its Byzantine offshoot as well, adopted Christianity as the official religion, a radical shift in church-state relations occurred. Christianity was now supported by the state, which had only shortly before persecuted it. In following centuries, as fortunes of pope and emperor rose and fell, the political influence and power of the ecclesiastical hierarchy of the church waxed and waned.

The Protestant Reformation in its main lines added little to church-state relations since the principal solution was to allow each state to follow the religion of its ruler, dissenting individuals having the right of emigration to a state whose religion they approved. The leftwing of the Reformation did produce a strong minority voice for the radical separation of church and state—a voice which gained weight as secular forces tended to move events in precisely that direction. A spirit of toleration toward religious minorities developed grudgingly. The trend toward toleration of dissent and disestablishment of religion was facilitated by a number of factors: the splintering of churches and sects with attendant political weakening of all the divided parties, widespread disgust at the toll of religious wars and feuds, a rapidly growing developmental understanding of religion with a consequent relativizing of religious claims, retreat of religion into private spirituality, and a mounting sense of the individual rights of men to choose their own beliefs.

It has often been emphasized, and rightly so, that many of these contributing factors toward political secularization were constructive and salutary not only for the state and society but for the church as well. The disestablishment of religion had two facets however: *institutional* separation of

136

church and state was accompanied by *ideological* separation of religion and politics. While the institutional separation has been wholly to the good, the ideological separation has had a decidedly mixed result both for political man and for religious man. This will become clearer as we proceed.

In sum, Israelite-Jewish-Christian attitudes toward the state and modes of adjustment to it have shown baffling variety. It would not be historically easy or theologically proper to try to write a single formula for the church's relation to the nations. Nonetheless, a distinct persisting theme in the Jewish and Christian communities has been respect for the state, and not merely in order to seize or influence power or to avert persecution and disability. This respect for the state stems from the historically oriented faith of Jew and Christian, which has repeatedly seen political power as one important field of divine action in the world.

In the Israelite-prophetic view of history, God was the Lord of history in a specific way. He was not the One related abstractly to individuals as integers in an indiscriminate mass. He was the One who stood behind and within the world of men in their several specific historic functions and contexts.[20] For Isaiah of Jerusalem, he was Lord of the world dominated by Assyria in which Judah had independent political responsibility. For Jeremiah, he was Lord of the world as ruled by Babylon in which Judah had sharply limited but still genuine political options. For Isaiah of the exile, he was Lord of the world about to be mastered by Persia and in which Judah's active political role was to be surrendered to Cyrus, but its place as official mediator for the empire was assured. Of course Israel's God was more than a "king" whose interests and means were exclusively political, but it is striking that in each era of Israel's life the religious interpreters were characteristically readers of political events and movements.

Admittedly the emphasis in much biblical thought is on the destructive judgmental work of God with the nations, but that should not be read as a categorical negative evaluation of either the Jewish or the Gentile states. The political forms in which the people of God lived were often criticized, but prophecy did not condemn them as unnecessary or intrinsically repugnant to God. The imperial powers which often threatened Israel could be *agents of God's judgment*, but also they could readily be seen as *objects* of his judgment and even, as Isaiah of the exile discovered, *instruments of his grace*. Cyrus of Persia was "messiah," bearer of a kind of secular grace necessary to Israel's mission as the people of God.

The New Testament outlook is less constructive than the Old Testament but it is not doctrinairely restrictive and anti-political, as was the temper of the Dead Sea sect (see pp. 43-49). The thought of the early Christian church, while not as politically rich and explicit as prophecy, does not forbid positive appropriation of the old fundamentally constructive Israelite-prophetic view of the nations. The creation faith of old Israel is very strong in the New Testament but the strictly political aspects and implications of that faith were not spelled out at any length; the reason for the political terseness of the New Testament is obviously that first-century conditions did not give Christians opportunity to express their faith politically.[21] Extrapolation from the spirit of the New Testament as seen in the light of Israelite prophecy is necessary to get a balanced directive for the church today.

It is not to be disputed that the New Testament witness

138

stands between the prophets of ancient Israel and our day so securely and crucially that we can never appropriate the Old Testament prophets simplistically. The sense of distance between God's work in the church and his work in the nation is widened by the New Testament perspective, but the seeming departure from Israelite prophecy was only relative and not absolute. The loosening up of the naïve identification of the whole visible Israel as faithful Israel began with the prophets and was intensified by Jesus. Yet neither Jesus nor his first followers broke the bond altogether any more than the prophets had; they looked forward to the enlarging of the true Israel to include Jews and pagans.[22] The apocalyptic element in the New Testament is not exclusive or all-determining, since the old wisdom and prophetic elements show an astonishing tenacity, coexisting with apocalyptic and refusing to be digested or intimidated by its flamboyant symbolism.[23]

It is essential, however, to guard against one damaging mistake that proponents of the continuity of biblical outlook on politics have frequently made. Under no circumstances can the people of God be identified with any one nation or alliance on the present scene; to do so is to saddle one's interpretation with the burden of unwieldy impracticality and of theological distortion. Outright equations between alliance politics in the ancient Near East and the twentieth century—for example, identifications of Babylon with Nazi Germany or Soviet Russia and of Israel with the United States or the West—are discredited efforts to find quick formulas in international affairs and have the effect of turning the covenant-creation orientation of the church's faith into mechanistic soothsaying in the service of intolerable self-righteousness. By way of contrast, there is a

139

legitimate and urgent task for biblical interpreters to suggest clues and perspectives drawn from prophecy which will help to illuminate the fully human and ecumenical urgencies of current politics.[24]

This means that the prophetic function of ancient Israel as the people of God is taken up by synagogue and church, not by any theocratic or quasi-sacral state, such as modern Israel or the United States. When the single prophet or the church as prophet speaks to the nation or state, the addressee is not the covenant people but man under the aspect of creation. Whatever the church says to man in society and to man within the state cannot be based on the assumption that society and state are answerable to a specifically Christian faith and ethic (or Jewish faith and ethic). What the church declares is the claim of the good as accessible to everyone who will examine himself and the political context. It seeks to awaken the latent sense of the intrinsically good or to probe for the functionally good which can be found as a dimension of creation. To short-circuit the process by speaking to the nation or state in explicit Jewish-Christian norms is to pay too little tribute either to Christ and his church (or Torah and synagogue) or to the wider world which God made and in which he is continually active, whether one thinks in terms of natural law or of functionalism.

Such a way of reading the relation between redemptive and natural communities recognizes that church and nation are two distinct but not sealed-off "orders," "realms," or "dimensions." The roles and mandates of the two cannot be interchanged or confused but they cannot be sundered either; their intimate relation stems from the fact that both are under the will of God, and all members of the church are also members of national bodies.

The difference between church and nation should be preserved in the church's refusal to impose its insights, ethics, or political dicta upon the nation or society by legal or nonlegal coercion. The intimate interconnection of church and nation should be expressed in the church's openness to the divine activity throughout all the levels of society and state and by the sustained noncoercive summons of the church to the nation that it carry out its natural functions in providing peace and order for human life.

Translated into domestic policy, this means that the church will be concerned with the broad range of issues in which human welfare is involved—and potentially that signifies all issues. But such involvement is very different from the church supplying a dogmatic solution for issues. Historically church and synagogue have commonly been alerted to domestic issues in the manner of any lobbying or pressure group.[25] They have shown interest and emotional involvement in direct proportion to some immediate institutional or dogmatic threat, e.g., birth control to Catholics, gambling to Protestants, minority discrimination to Jews. Such a limited response is sociologically completely understandable but theologically and ethically inexcusable and deplorable.

The church, in its Jewish and Christian forms, is that people which symbolizes redeemed humanity and which must see itself as the constant advocate of human welfare. It must recognize its involvement not only on matters that pose direct threats to religious institutions or dogmas, or even on such obvious "moral" matters as civil rights, but also in more complicated and "secular" matters such as education,

141

automation, urban renewal, automobile safety, public transportation, medical care, dope addiction, and crime. In other words, the domestic political and social responsibility of the church is not defined by those issues that can be solved by political or religious slogans or offhand formulas. As a matter of fact, very few such problems exist any more, if they ever did. All social and political problems are now to a large extent technical problems; they are problems that enlist the cooperative involvement of many skills and insights.[26] It is precisely the old Israelite historic sense of contingent revelation and responsibility that gives the church the mandate and the resources to work in the technical pragmatic sphere. In so doing the church must surrender the all too tempting dogmatic temper which tends to prescribe answers for the human situation from somewhere out of the past or form somewhere in the theoretical heavens.

In foreign affairs, church and synagogue must stand sufficiently apart from the nation that they can bring constructive criticism to bear upon the inevitable egocentricity of the state's foreign policies. Churches and synagogues have been notoriously uncritical of the foreign policies of their respective countries and, in many cases, have been belligerently chauvinistic, thereby reverting to a naïve subprophetic view of the church as merging with and validating the nation in which it lives. At other times, the church has advanced theoretically vague or inapplicable panaceas, for example, absolute pacifism, for a state that is unable or unwilling to follow such a course.[27]

The burden of Jew or Christian, when he approaches foreign affairs, is to examine the relative claims of the various contending states with a view to introducing reason and flexibility in a field where passion and rigidity have fre-

142

quently held sway. The church has a special historic obligation at this point inasmuch as a good measure of the former religious fanaticism, which inspired Christian pogroms against Jews and pitted Catholics against Protestants and vice versa, has now migrated to political affairs. In fact the mark of a doctrinaire communist or a hard-line anticommunist is precisely his quasi-religious self-assurance and zealous impulse to demolish opposing devils, apostates, and heretics. The church must seek in its respective national settings to "de-fuse" these fanaticisms by drawing on its own traditional resources, especially its long view on national animosities and its prophetic faith in the relativity of nations, combined with a relevant analysis of the current data of international life, which so often contradict absolutist communism and anticommunism. For church and synagogue in the West there is the particular task of assuring that one absolutist target of hatred and fear is not simply exchanged for another, for example, in the present mellowing of attitude toward Russia associated with a hardening of attitude toward China.

In recent years the maturity and effectiveness of church and synagogue in America, both theologically and socially, have been mightily tested by the civil rights movement.[28] In spite of considerable public fanfare and many individual contributions far beyond the call of duty, the religious bodies as a whole are still remote from the movement—not so much hostile as ungripped and uninvolved. A creative "remnant" has made astounding strides in securing important "breakthroughs" on many civil rights fronts. But for minorities to be fully accepted in our society, and for the church to vindicate its own heritage and vocation, a vastly wider involvement of Jews and Christians in the aspirations

143

and efforts of Negroes, Puerto Ricans, Mexicans, and Indians will be required. A battle that has been largely legal and symbolic will have to become a battle for housing, employment and education and, finally, a battle for the reconstitution of the dignity and identity of minorities—in short, black power. These are battles in which privileged Jews and Christians will join one way or another; if mass nonparticipation by advantaged Jews and Christians continues we can expect the battles to be far more violent and disruptive than they need be. As has been noted for Americans in general, it may be singularly said of Jews and Christians, "if they were to save themselves and restore democracy, [they] would have to stop signing names and put themselves on the dotted line." [29]

In international affairs, the war in Vietnam offers an urgent challenge to the church and the synagogue. There are even possibilities that they could join their concerns and resources with those of Buddhists, the other religious group most directly involved in Vietnam. It is of particular importance that the church not be put off by the fact that some of the most vocal critics of the American war in Vietnam are totally pacifist in orientation or seem to have no sense of Marxist totalitarianism. Relevant Jewish-Christian political analysis will not be able to begin with pacifism by fiat for the state, but the religious legitimacy of pacifism will certainly have to be explored and nonviolent methods of defense and international problem-solving will be encouraged in order to test their military and political feasibility.[30] Also, relevant Jewish-Christian political analysis of foreign affairs will not want to whitewash communist evils in Vietnam, or elsewhere; it will insist, however, that the wrongs of communism not be used as a cloak to avoid honest comparison of respective wrongs and even as a legitimation for any sort of heavy-handed political and military policies by the West. It will even be willing to face the possibility that in Vietnam, the National Liberation Front, in spite of its communist coloration, offers the people a better future than does the United States in tandem with the largely upper-class, antireform Saigon government.[31]

More and more, discussions about "wars of liberation" will turn on historical rather than dogmatic considerations. It will be less a question of whether one side is wholly right or wholly wrong. It will be more an assessment of the appropriateness (morally, politically, militarily, socially) of various kinds of outside involvement (whether by single powers or by regional and international bodies) in the light of the complex of political and social realities in the country. Means and ends will be related at every step. What the people of the divided country actually want and think will be more important than whether they are "communist" or "anticommunist."

Generally, opposition to America's conduct in Vietnam by religiously based critics does not repudiate United States concern to act for freedom or contend that communists in Vietnam are merely innocent reformers. The criticism is that America's particular actions do not serve freedom and justice on the local scene and that the communist totalitarian element in the revolt is not as significant as the nationalist-socialist protest against imperial interference (by French, Japanese, Americans) and entrenched feudalism and oligarchism (by the Saigon governments).

To put it bluntly, honest Jewish-Christian thought cannot simply take the cold war as the starting point and touchstone of all else in the analysis of foreign affairs. The cold war must remain only one factor among many others. It is not to be assumed that wherever communists are involved, the cause they support is automatically wrong and the opposing cause or force is automatically right. What Vietnam seems to be showing is that in a given situation the local aims and means of a strongly communist-penetrated movement, even a communist-controlled movement, may be relatively more just—even somewhat "freer"!—than the aims and means of the noncommunist forces allied against change. Moreover, if the worthiness of the aims and means of the contending parties in Vietnam are in serious doubt, so that no one can discern the patterns of justice with any confidence, the massive insertion of foreign forces may be just the factor that tips the balance toward the side of those whose movement remains largely indigenous.

The church's function in assessing America's foreign policies is perhaps best illustrated by a single example. Most Americans have little difficulty in seeing that the French in Algeria were, and the Portuguese in Angola and Mozambique are, fighting repressive and mistaken wars against political and social forces that will eventually prevail. In Algeria the resolution was eased by France's eventual unilateral withdrawal from the war in favor of independence for the country. The church must help the American people to face the question: Is American involvement in Vietnam different from French involvement in Algeria and Portuguese involvement in Angola? [32] In other words, the church as the historic people of God must assist citizens of a nation to gain some emotional distance from its own involvements and to assess them realistically, not piously, in the light of the total human welfare which will of course include the nation's own highest good.

146

At the extreme boundary of the church's involvement in domestic and foreign affairs are acts of conscientious protest and dissent. By themselves these acts do not solve problems, which must be dealt with constructively and arduously in other ways. But acts of conscience may serve to caution against hasty or wrong solutions or against obstructive actions that impede or prevent solutions. No honest civil rights worker believes that public demonstrations will by themselves secure minority rights and achieve racial harmony. No sane peace worker expects that public protests or open refusals to support the war in Vietnam will by themselves bring peace to Southeast Asia. Sometimes, however, the point in nations is reached—and not only in some other time or place, such as Nazi Germany—when dissent is the only immediate course available to critics and when the very public dissent clears the air for discussion and crystallizes alternatives.

The church-based protest against foreign policy will nonetheless have failed crucially if it does not strike deeper roots than those of opposition and negation. At this point the old Israelite prophetic models are of inestimable value to the church. Negative as the prophets were on many issues, they searched at all times for a deep common level of national consensus. They expressed and yearned for an enduring unity which prevented their opposition from becoming querulous divisiveness. Hysteria or opportunism did not lure them, nor did exhibitionism indulge their neglected egos. The prophets grieved for and contended with their people, trying all the while to reach agreement with them on a common life purified of ethnocentricity.

It is a source of continual astonishment to this writer that the traditional resources of Judaism and Christianity supply

147

such a vast but untapped reservoir of insight and motivation for building an international political community. We have seen in the old Israelite faith, and continuing on into Judaism and Christianity, a belief that nations in their freedom will find unity and harmony under the divine will. The urgent need for the revision or replacement of the United Nations so as to create a carefully limited but genuinely effective international problem-solving apparatus is transparent to intelligent people everywhere. No single nation has yet demonstrated the traditional resources or the requisite objectivity to spearhead the task. Jews and Christians—and perhaps adherents of other religions—have the traditions and may yet develop the objectivity to contribute toward the building of a limited nontotalitarian worldwide government that will eliminate extralegal force from world affairs. The task of constructing and gaining consent for such a government, in spite of all the technical political difficulties, is fundamentally a psychological and theological one. That is to say, the vital technical pragmatic considerations will only be tackled and seen through to conclusion when the will to peaceful unity is stronger and more tenacious than the counterwill to destructive isolation and unilateral action.

The peace vocation of church and synagogue today is, therefore, far from exhausted in confronting Vietnam or the cold war. The church's peace vocation is a call to involvement in the political coming-of-age of a world either about to make the last great stride to international war-control or to fall back into chaos. It is a vocation which proceeds side by side with the effort to bring full freedom to minorities everywhere, and not least in America. It is the endeavor to attain for all nations the right to exist and to settle their problems with outside help but without outside coercion and, finally, to secure for the citizens of all countries a full, dignified life. Realistically that is a vocation for the coming centuries, but substantive advances must be made in the next decade and generation if the races against nuclear war, thought conformity and control, population explosion, etc., are seriously to be entered, much less won.

The calling of the church vis-à-vis the nations is not to add to its membership or to earn a good reputation for itself. Its calling is to assist the nations to fulfill their own proper functions to the benefit of the human race. It is the highest form of ecumenism, albeit a chastened secular ecumenism. Church and nation alike must in a fashion decrease; the human race, in its several specific historic needs and grasped as a unity, must increase.

## D. THE CHURCH'S FAITH AND
## THE CULTURE WITHIN AND WITHOUT

WE have tried to let the biblical faith speak for itself and, in doing so, to speak to some of the crucial church-culture issues of the present. Inevitably our choice of what is central in the Bible has been selective but hopefully neither peripheral nor idiosyncratic. Similarly, our assessment of the status of the church today has been selective but again hopefully authentic and recognizable to many readers. Certainly the main thrust of the biblical and contemporary analyses is not merely the writer's private view. He has attempted to speak for a significant segment of the church, especially among the younger clergy and laity. His points of view are arguable but, if they are wrong or onesided, it will not be due to isolation from Bible, church, or culture. If anything, faults and deficiencies will most likely stem from too close a proximity to a rapidly changing theological and cultural situation. In any event, however, it is in this telescoped and kaleidoscopic situation that we all must make our decisions and select our priorities. The test of the contributions offered here will be whether they assist contemporary Christians in correlating biblical thought and current church-in-world decisions.

The key concept of this study is the correlation between the church as the historically covenanted people of God and culture as the human world where God's work is real but less focused—i.e., less discernible—than in the church.

It was proposed provisionally in the introduction (p. 13). that the church as the people of God refers to the community of men from Moses to the present who have experienced, confessed, and attempted to live out the reality of communion or covenant with God. It designates Jews and Christians. It entails both the primal personal and communal root experience as well as the consequent forms of worship and communal order, the laws and mores developed within historic Jewish and Christian bodies. It embraces a quality of faith and a pattern of life.

Let us now explore this understanding by underlining the notion of mutuality and reciprocity in the dynamics of the church.[33] Authentic church consciousness always recognizes the initiating movement of God toward man and the responding movement of man to God. In biblical terms, God "chooses" or "elects" a people and enters into "covenant" with them, a bond in which gratitude and love are expressed in obedience. The church springs up as a meeting of God and man through spatio-temporal media and in constantly changing events and structures. The fundamental medium for the Jew is Torah, for the Christian Jesus of Nazareth. There are extremely significant differences involved in the two media but structurally they both present an "election-covenant" or "grace-faith" pattern based on historical encounter, with cultic and metaphysical acts and symbols playing important but secondary roles.

There is always a tendency in the church's life and thought to domesticate or to freeze the dynamism of God's impact upon man, to talk more about past than about present and future, in fact to *talk about* God rather than to *take part in* what God is doing or about to do. There is always an inclination for the confessor of the biblical God to assume that he at any rate knows how God is acting, even though most men are wide of the mark. This constitutional bias toward prejudging, limiting, classifying, and thus depreciating the action of God is a form of unbelief, or perhaps we should say a too confident "overbelief," that has to be overcome by every fresh occurrence of God's act in human life. The church is never once for all; it is always springing to life before our surprised eyes.

We have seen how ancient Israel's historical communion with God was repeatedly threatened and compromised by gross and subtle misunderstandings. It is astonishing how often basically similar misunderstandings infect synagogue and church today. Perhaps the most frequent corruptions of church-consciousness are those which tend to define the church as a morally superior people, as God's only people, or as a professedly or intrinsically religious people. Let us evaluate each in turn.

In the first place, the church does not denote a morally superior people. The church is not composed of those who are worthy of divine honor, people who—in contrast to others—deserve to be God's. The goodness that belongs to God's people is either the common goodness familiar in all creation in spite of man's alienation from God or it is the good work of God through the historical covenant on our behalf. The serious demands for righteousness of life, which appear throughout the Bible, stand under the prior truth that God has created the possibility of righteousness by drawing the covenant circle within which we may stand in spite of our frailty.

Second, the church does not refer to God's only people.

The covenant relationship is unique, but it is not closed or limited in the sense that those who belong to the church are not the only people loved and ruled by God; in fact, to be among God's people, in the sense of conscious participation in his purposes, is to be acutely aware of the universality of the divine compassion and of the divine dominion. If the covenant circle includes *me* in spite of *my* limitations and rebellion, in principle and in intent it includes *everyone*.

Third, the church is not limited to a professedly or intrinsically religious people. God's people are not those who happen to be of a more pious or ecclesiastical bent than other men. They are not extrovert "joiners" and compulsive "organization men." Though they should know better by now, churchmen are inclined to forget that the church is not simply to be equated with activities carried on within a sacral building or under the auspices of a formally religious organization. God's people are those who stand within the circle of his covenant and who find themselves joyously and awesomely compelled to live the whole of their lives in the light of covenant. God's people are his people just as they are and wherever they are, in their homes and jobs, their sports and love-making, their eating and warring, fully as much as in formal religious activities. In fact, there are times when being the church means challenging what passes for the church, even dissociating oneself from it or from some of its effete and debased expressions.

In describing such perennial debasements of the church we are admitting that the church stands in the tension between human weakness and divine grace. We never pass beyond the enigma of the inadequacy of the church, which is nevertheless called to be God's instrument. We never

153

shake free of the obligation that rests upon the church to cling less selfishly to its privilege and tradition and to consider more faithfully the love of God for his world. It is patent that, as biblically conceived, the church could only arise at all where men experienced their weakness overcome, their rebellion forgiven, their divisions healed—but always from beyond themselves. The church is a means for the divine grace to manifest itself in the whole of human life, but the church is a *means of grace* only insofar as it is the *consequence of grace*. So then the church is always a servant concept—from one to another—or a bridge concept—from here to there—while God, man, history, society are the realities to be interconnected; the kingdom of God brackets the church as it brackets the nation.

Our whole way of discerning "church" in ancient Israel and in the present context has had a double character. "Church" always has a historical, communal character, marked by specific memories and symbols (centrally the Torah or Jesus Christ). "Church" also always has a dynamic, eventful character, marked by specific discoveries of God's action in the present and commitment to it (the precise way in which Torah or Jesus confronts us). "Church" has continuity and contextuality, tradition and novelty, assurance and precariousness, visibility and invisibility. "Church" is historically shaped and history-shaping.

For the relation of church to culture it is particularly important to explore this warp and woof of the church's fabric, so as to see how the church's visibility and invisibility are related and what we can actually expect of these two paradoxical marks of the church. We must see if possible how their balanced combination can guide us on the present uncharted sea of church-culture interchange.

There has been a long and honorable theological tradition about "the church visible" and "the church invisible." It has never been a simple conception but has developed many strands and nuances. In Reformation theology at least four of these stand out: (1) reference to the double aspect of the true church, invisible insofar as its essence is fellowship by faith with Christ in the Holy Spirit, but visible insofar as it always finds outward expression in the preaching of the word and the celebration of the sacraments (Luther); (2) reference to the discrepancy between Christian profession and Christian faith, visible referring to the church which includes hypocrites, invisible referring to the body of true believers which lies within the visible church (Luther; Calvin); (3) reference to the distinction between the church particular or visible in a given place and the church universal or invisible in that no man can experience it empirically in its entirety (Zwingli; Calvin); (4) reference to the distinction between the invisible church as the sum total of the elect who will become manifest only at the end of history and the visible church which includes both the church universal and the church particular (Zwingli; Calvin).[34] While serving many purposes, these several understandings come together in the agreement that the true church cannot be simply equated with the living members of particular congregations.

But theology is always more than what theologians teach; it involves the popular folkways that cling to the teachings and eventually overgrow them unless new theological correction arises. The theological tension of church visible and church invisible became the folkway division between the church material and the church spiritual. As the two categories fell apart, the material was denigrated and the spiritual was elevated, thereby seriously attenuating the biblical recognition of God's activity as Creator and Redeemer within his world. Especially on the American scene, with its strong free-church tradition, the visibility of the church has become its voluntary and discrete character as an organization of persons somewhat randomly related to God and to one another, just as "matter" is only loosely related to "spirit." The invisibility of the church has become, on the one hand, the privacy of the religious life within the unseen inner realms of man; and, on the other, the otherworldliness of faith that touches only what is spiritual in man and therefore is communicated nonobjectively and emotionally to each believer.

Once the dissolution of church visible and church invisible into bifurcated realms is well advanced, destructive results begin to appear in the form of theological vapidity (since the very invisibility and personal character of faith lead to its inarticulateness), institutional rigidity (in which, ironically, the supposedly indifferent or at least optional forms of the visible church become a matter of urgency for defining and preserving the church), and social and cultural irrelevance (since invisible and atomistic faith does not need to face the issues of man's visible life).

It is obvious that the classic Reformation insights into the church visible and the church invisible contain much of contemporary value, but they cannot be directly appropriated without bearing in mind the widespread attending corruptions that more often pervade the church than do the clarifying insights. It is also clear that the Reformation distinctions are entwined in the way of putting and answering theological questions that marked the sixteenth century and which cannot be taken for granted as immediately applicable today.[35] We must try to put the nature of the church's visibility and invisibility in a way that will build upon the biblical understanding, take Reformation and other theologies into account, and yet a way which will speak with clarity to the present position of the church.

A conception of church visibility and invisibility might be grasped today along the lines of the biological model of an *organism* [36] (which is, interestingly, already foreshadowed in the New Testament symbol of the church as the Body of Christ). The church may be regarded as an organism in these respects: (1) it is a specific body in that it is composed of persons, past, present, and future; (2) it is a composite body of many members or organs bound together in infinite metabolic complexity, in contrast to a collection of disparate elements; (3) it is a continuing, maturing body with an identity over against its environment, but one which develops in responses and adjustments to its environment. It persists through the passage of time and the vicissitudes of environment but it is what it is by virtue of the time in which it has matured and the environment that has nurtured and shaped it. As in biology, so in ecclesiology: the respective roles of heredity and environment, of revelation and humanization, cannot be simply assessed; they are in fact different perspectives on the same organic reality.

One value of describing the church organically is that it preserves the historically tangible and ongoing character of the church but also avoids the gross error of regarding the institutional church as the total church, when in fact it is not more than the skeletal structure or, in given cases, a vestigial growth or a discarded skin. Or, perhaps more aptly, the organism of the church will have many different morphologies suited to its several temporal or spatial environments. It will always have a form, the institution will always be there, but it will be adaptable and will grow out of the organism's confrontation with the challenges in its current environment. An organic sense of the church transcends but also accounts for the institutional church, liberating it so that it may be the truly plastic and serviceable form that it must be if it is "to keep up with God," so to speak.

Another value of conceiving the church organically is to put a brake on church provincialism, to caution against making the church coterminous with the whole activity and purpose of God. For one thing, the church in its *organic visibility* is not coterminous with God's total purpose because it is still in process; the organism is not yet complete and mature. For another, the church in its *organic totality* is not coterminous with the entire purpose of God because his purpose runs through the many other organisms of human life which do not have the specific historical focus of Torah or Jesus Christ. Morever, the divine purpose catches up the nonhuman realms of creation and possibly also other universes of men or personal beings. In other words, the church is not the Kingdom of God but participates in and gives concrete expression to the Kingdom of God. Even when the church will have lived out its purpose, it will not thereby have "built" or "brought" the Kingdom except as it has served its limited role in God's total work. Other organisms and roles in culture and nature will have had their part to play in the ordering of the rule of God.

In effect then, several of the valid insights of the Reformers with respect to the church's visibility and invisibility can be reformulated today in terms of the biological model of organism. There is, however, another aspect, which was not appreciated by the Reformers, in fact one not ade-

158

quately appreciated by churchmen and theologians until this century. It is an element of churchly invisibility that we have noted in the biblical traditions but which, even there, tends to be submerged under a surface emphasis upon the community of Israel or the early church.

The church's invisibility not only refers to the way the historical people of God work quietly in their dispersed roles in society or in their family circles. The church's invisibility also refers to the activity of men in culture at large, which is in the character of the church but which is not consciously identified with the historic church. Some of these men may be adherents of nonhistorical or noncovenantal religions. Others may be nominal or inactive members of the confessing church. Still others may be conscious rebels who have deliberately separated from the visible church. Finally, many may be thoroughgoing secularists who have never put human questions in any theological way or they may be outright agnostics and atheists who have rejected theological or confessional categories after some sort of attempt to understand them.

What we are saying is that the church invisible is not formed exclusively of Christians and Jews who consciously live their faith in society. We are saying that nominal Christians and Jews, ex-Christians and ex-Jews, followers of other faiths, secularists, agnostics, and atheists may all take part in churchly actions. By this we mean that they advance the humanization of society in a way faithful to the best insights of the historic visible church. They are genuinely involved in the process of humanization, understood in largely or exclusively immanental and empirical categories, part of the same process which the church conceives as human redemption or salvation, understood in largely symbolic categories derived from her own special history. Both are concerned with right human relations in an ongoing historical context, with reference to certain worthy ends which cannot be separated from the means to their advancement. Humanization may be more concerned with means than ends; redemption may be more concerned with ends than means. For either perspective to have meaning, however, both ends and means must be correlated, albeit in necessarily different realms of discourse: humanization in the technical-empirical realm and redemption in the symbolic-historical realm. It is the task of the church visible to bring these realms closer together in practice and thought.[37]

For a mature doctrine of the church today, full place must be given to the church within culture, the crypto-church, or the anonymous church, in which God is as validly and actively at work as in the historically or covenantally defined church. This is not to say that the distinctions between historic church and crypto-church are unimportant, any more than it is appropriate to erase distinctions between the covenantal and the noncovenantal religions. It is to insist, however, that the crypto-church must be reckoned with as a major instrument of God, one that the church in its historic embodiment cannot ignore and with which it must increasingly ally itself for various kinds of immediate and long-range study and action. Social action as something that a church committee or individual members do on the periphery of the congregation will give way to the conception of social action as something God and men do in concert throughout human life; some activities will be initiated from within the institutional church, but many more will arise in culture on other institutional foundations, and with all of them the church must come to theological and practical terms as a congregation and not simply as individual believers.

So we shall now try to sketch the way in which the Israelite church-culture patterns work out in the present church climate, with particular attention to the issues of the church's visibility and invisibility.

*Demarcation.* The church is always taking shape, continually being formed and sustained by God's action among men and for men. The Christian church is not defined by anything more specific than Jesus and the complex of history and tradition leading to him and flowing from him. The history and tradition are themselves radically subservient to the core-reality of history-making communion with God and they are frankly alterable and multiply applicable to the always emerging novelty of the moment. The forms of church life familiar to a given period, denomination, region, class, or party that tend to survive by sheer inertia and to appear so immutable (e.g., Sunday school, colonial architecture, residential parish!) are subject to change and even to disposal whenever the church is radically demarcated in contrast to the easygoing mass production of culture Christians.

The sharpest way to put the substance of the church's demarcation is to say that the church is that community which (1) recognizes the God who acted in Torah and in Jesus as the God who is presently acting, and (2) orders its life collectively and individually by participation in the present activity of God.

*Outreach and Incorporation.* The demarcation is authentic only if the aspect of God's present work is made central. The church which remembers Jesus becomes open toward events and movements, crises and processes in which

161

the God of Jesus is seen at work portentously in destruction and reconciliation. The church puts its finger on the world's pulse; it locates the persons and events and forces which are catalytic for setting the reality of the church into motion. It is an alert mood, watching for God's action in sometimes opaque and resistant sources; it is equally a relaxed mood, since the church rightly demarcated need not be anxious about how God's action proceeds, whether within or outside of the prescribed religious channels. The church will try to discern the direction of God's moves by means of a constant interplay between the historical paradigms (Jesus and Torah) and the novel present (the pragmatic structures and demands of present existence). It will not capitulate to a "don't-rock-the-boat" status quo mentality. It will sense that God is always rocking the boat of human affairs; the question will be: in which of the increasingly changeful dimensions of human life is God portentously and demandingly at work? Portentously, for how is God really working toward a new and better future for man? Demandingly, for what is the part that men must play in his work, particularly those men who remember his work of old? The outreaching and incorporating church, therefore, will not be grabbing at mere novelty, nor will it be tricked into reading more into social and political disturbances than is there. It will seek for the depth and direction of the disturbances, for the human possibilities that are thwarted or liberated in the disturbances.

*Attraction.* There is also a movement of the world toward the church. This may not seem to be a potent factor in church-culture relations today, but it is operative and it has its opportunities and dangers.

One of the ever present perils is that the archaic or highly specialized culture-world of the church may attract refugees of lost cultures for nostalgic or reactionary reasons. The cultural aura surviving from an earlier stage of the church's history may appeal to men who want anchorage in solid symbols and institutions. There is a deceptively thin but actually sharp line between seeking in the church resources to face any culture and seeking in the church solace for a culture that is past. Where the church offers a culture-surrogate so that people feel less responsible for wise change in the wider culture it becomes a theological and cultural fossil or monstrosity instead of a healthy organism.

From another direction the church may be sought for what it can do strategically toward preserving or serving particular interests or toward effecting social change. In this case stress is not on meeting the psychic and cultural needs of individuals but on the church's ideological or structural suitability to resist or to effect change. In some cases what is to be preserved or changed may on balance be desirable, and the church as an institution will wish to have its part. It will, however, be best for all concerned to realize the strictly partial and provisional nature of the alliance and not to mistake the immediate conjunction of interests for conversion to the historical faith of the church, on the one side, or diminution of the confession of the church, on the other. In each case the criterion for judging participation in causes must be the activity of God as best the committed church can discern it. The church is freed from compulsive calculation about its doctrinal purity, or its institutional image or convenience, and can decide about each challenge in terms of human interests in the light of the history-making communion with God.

Yet this theologically guarded openness toward the world

of culture is not cynically or provincially determined. As soon as the church takes seriously its own paradigms it knows that God is at work here and now. It knows that God's work is hidden and paradoxical. Inasmuch as the church is in no position to know fully in advance how God's action will take shape, it will be open to the gestures of culture at every point, straining to catch a clear sign of what God is doing. This kind of trust in God as Lord of culture makes the church content to coexist with other types of cultural forms and institutions and even to be penetrated by them and to take on cultural concerns as its own concerns. It will be exceedingly sensitive to academic, scientific-technological, bureaucratic, artistic, and minority culture tensions and developments. It will receive the inquiries, however vague, and the attacks, however hostile, from spokesmen for these cultural segments—both in the person of church members and of outsiders. The mood of the church which attracts culture will not be one of anxious transformation of cultural issues into ecclesiastical or dogmatic issues; by letting them stand as genuine cultural issues they become theological issues, i.e., they become questions about how God is acting to humanize life in our world and what is inhibiting his action. The mood of the attracting church will be a basically receptive, trusting, although not uncritical, mood which will convey to culture-involved man, within and without the church, that his questions and decisions are basic for grasping the form of God's action today.

*Approximation.* Undoubtedly the most difficult phase of church-culture relations is the church's actual acceptance of its limited and provisional character. The consequence of God being hidden is that the church is also hidden. As previously argued, the invisibility of the church points in part to

164

the fact that church-functions and church-characteristics are often at work in culture. Culture contains as a continuous potentiality, a crypto-church, which cannot be grounds for disbanding the confessing church, but which also cannot be reduced to the confessing church or ranked hierarchically beneath it (see pp. 91-95).

Doubtless one of the key features of our age is that increasingly the confessing church and the crypto-church are recognizing their essential brotherhood. That culture can perform churchly functions, can be the locus of the judging-reconciling work of God, has been granted in theory by confessing church and synagogue. The implementation of the theoretical possibility has been, however, normally grudging and woefully late, often years and decades—even centuries—late.

If the concept of the culture's approximation to church is to make any sense, it cannot be taken as a quantitative assertion but must be taken as *an assertion about perspective and function*. It is to speak of a way of looking at culture and understanding its operations. It is to be alert to the way in which culture serves to humanize life (i.e., to enrich, diversify, deepen, liberate human relations) rather than to dehumanize it (i.e., standardize, impoverish, constrict, reify human relations). It is to be able to recognize that one of the ways God works is precisely in and through the process of humanization, which is a work of culture.

A perspective of this sort is not, then, mainly interested in defining the causes and organizations which have a divine seal of approval. To do so is to imply that God is not at work in other causes and organizations or that the approved causes and organizations can do no wrong. Both are fallacies. The civil rights revolution may be church. Community or-

165

ganization of the poor may be church. Centers for dope addicts and alcoholics may be church. Student activities to gain constitutional rights on campus and to acquire a significant share in educational policy-making may be church. Teach-ins on Vietnam and civil disobedience against the war may be church. But they are all church in the same dynamic, provisional way that the institutional church is. To baptize them too flatly is to fail to retain critical judgment and thus to fail to be open to God's own revolutionary activity. It is equally essential to be open to what alternative causes and movements represent, for in them too God is saying something, perhaps less directly translatable but nonetheless urgent. What renovations and renewals are needed in culture may become especially clear in assessing totalitarian political movements, the industrial-military complex, minority riots, white backlash, militant anticommunism, American interventionism abroad. Only by encountering the full force of these movements and realities can we appreciate the public decisions and policies inspired by ignorance and prejudice which public officials are unwilling or unable to resist although, personally, they know better.

Communism itself will be more faithfully probed by the church in order to discover the meaning of God's revolutionary action. The crippling and hardening effects of the cold war and McCarthyism on American economic and social thought will have to be consciously counteracted by a truly responsible church. It will not be enough to issue timid pronouncements on accommodation with communist countries. It will be incumbent on the church to trace the various strands that have gone into the making of communist societies and states, and that will require many distinc-

166

tions not now commonly made. On the political level, it will be necessary to distinguish between communism that is imperialistically aggressive and communism that is content to work by persuasion, between communism imposed in a one-party state and communism that is subject to the elective will of the populace. On the social and economic level it will be necessary to distinguish between pure Marxist theory and the state capitalism of Soviet Russia, between the urge to a radical democratic Socialism appearing in many younger communists and the stodgy conformism of established communist bureaucracies.

It will have to be asked how far the political, social, and economic forms of life in communist and noncommunist countries approximate the conditions for the true humanization of men. If on the whole noncommunist countries show a far better record on the political level than do the communist countries, in social and economic matters some communist societies, or at least aspects of those societies, will probably offer more favorable conditions for human growth than some noncommunist societies. The key to the whole analysis will be a loosening of crude ideological strictures, permitting movement away from simpleminded "procommunist" and "anticommunist" stances in which the respective critics and defenders are obligated to predictable role-playing.

The historic church can assist in the task of de-ideologizing the relations between communists and noncommunists, but to do so it will be necessary to destroy the myth of communists as godless men and noncommunists as believers. Recognition of the crypto-church will make this liberation from cold-war ideology possible: communists too may do the work of God, and not only in negative judgment, but in positive construction as well. It is of interest that one Yugoslavian communist can describe a true democratic socialism (communism) as Christian socialism, "not because the free democratic Socialist society would profess the Christian faith, but because the projection of authentic Christianity into the sociopolitical sphere is democracy." [38] Of late some Spanish and Italian communist theoreticians have urged a closer alliance of communists and Catholics to bring about social change.[39] The alliance they describe is not the older Marxist type of temporary alliance of convenience but a continuing mixture of cooperation and competition based on the assumptions that communism and Catholicism have some things in common and that their respective values can best be tested in social reconstruction. Such points of view represent a considerable advance beyond Marx's curt dismissal of Christianity as a religious projection of reactionary economics.

The central discovery of this study has been that the biblical understanding of the church in tension and communication with culture is a necessary paradigm for the church today in its relations with culture. We have had ample occasion to note how subtle and complex are church-culture dynamics. In particular we have had to face the constant appearance of culture within the church and church within the culture in such an interrelationship that new theological forms and ecclesiastical and social-action patterns will have to develop if the church is not to be left stranded with a style of life and thought that is hopelessly outmoded.

We have said much about church as a demarcating, humanizing reality in culture. One final word about culture as a focusing, institutionalizing reality in the church. Implicit in our analyses of ancient Israelite communal forms was the recognition that they were continually shaped by the larger cultural environment and were at the same time stamped by the central theological realities experienced in a given era. For the communal religious forms to remain alive and meaningful they had to be related correlatively to the socio-cultural context and to the contemporary theological experience. The perils in such a correlation were those either of clinging stubbornly to worn-out socio-cultural contexts and faded theological experiences or of misidentifying the current context and fabricating phony theological structures. In short, history-making communion with God might be turned into veneration of past history or speculation about theoretical history.

It is sometimes said that biblical faith cannot help us much at this point because it exhibited so many different cultural combinations. H. Richard Niebuhr reminds us that "Those critics of cultural Protestantism who urge return to Biblical ways of thought sometimes seem to forget that many cultures are represented in the Bible." [40] The criticism is tellingly correct for those who think that "biblical theology" entails a specific once-and-for-all church-culture correlation or that "faith" can be suspended above or especially protected within culture. But anyone who has taken the pains to penetrate the surface of the Bible will soon discover that the genius of its witness is that God is constantly making history by meeting men in changing churchly and cultural settings. Not an enduring finished synthesis of church and culture, nor a disembodied spirituality, but a way of reading church and culture as mutually interpenetrating

169

*dimensions of God's activity* is what the Bible should convey to us.

The practical result is that combined with the relative fixity of the past history and tradition of the church's witness goes a singularly open church-culture spectrum or series of interlocking church-culture spheres. The present believer in the history-making God of the Jewish and Christian communities does not stand securely on a fixed quantum called church, from which he can conveniently select cultural tidbits to his liking. He stands in the swirling vortex of contending and clashing church and culture claims. In company with his fellow believers he must seek to construct a tentative standing place in which he will have to recognize the formative humanizing work of God as coinciding at many points with the humanizing work of man. What will give him his security and direction will not be fixed forms of the church but the sense of continuity in the work of God who acted and who acts. The result is both an appreciable relativizing of the transcendent and an appreciable elevation of the empirical. Some fear that this will be fatal for a transcendent faith like Judaism or Christianity. It is far more likely to hasten the renewal of a faith whose genuinely historical and empirical face has often been masked by false transcendence. In any event, the human experience of our age is putting Judaism and Christianity to a radical test of their viability—whether we Jews and Christians choose to cooperate or not.

# NOTES

## PART I

1. YAHWEH is the proper name for the God of ancient Israel. It is translated as LORD in the Authorized Version and in the Revised Standard Version, and as JEHOVAH in the English Revised Version and in the American Standard Version. Wherever YAHWEH appears in the Hebrew Bible, the Jews now substitute ADONAI in reading the text. For fuller treatment, see B. W. Anderson, "God, names of," *IDB*, II (1962), pp. 409-411.

2. For the view that the Israelite concepts of the covenant were modeled on political vassal treaties, cf. G. Mendenhall, *Law and Covenant in Israel and the Ancient Near East* (1955) and updated in his article on "Covenant" in *IDB*, I (1962), pp. 714-723. D. McCarthy, *Treaty and Covenant* (1963), is much less convinced of the aptness of the comparison.

3. Extremely influential in awakening interest in the tribal league or amphictyony as the crucial formative period in Israelite history was M. Noth, *Das System der Zwoelf Staemme Israels* (1930). For his view in brief compass, cf. Noth, *The History of Israel* (1960), pp. 85-109.

4. Among recent synoptic treatments of prophecy which attempt to grapple with its theological outlook we may mention A. Heschel, *The Prophets* (1962); J. Lindblom, *Prophecy in Ancient Israel* (1962), chap. 5; B. Napier, *Prophets in Perspective* (1962), chap. 5.

5. R. Scott, *IB*, V (1956), pp. 231-234, 247-250 proposes that the messianic oracles of Isaiah, chaps. 9 and 11, be understood as coronation recitations, at least partly traditional in character, which Isaiah possibly held up to Israelite kings as reminders of their oaths to God and people.

6. Concerning the amazing breadth and detail in the political prophecy of Isaiah see N. Gottwald, *All the Kingdoms of the Earth. Israelite Prophecy and International Relations in the Ancient Near East* (1964), pp. 147-208.

7. E. Jacob, "The Biblical Prophets: Revolutionaries or Conservatives?" *Interpretation*, 19 (1965), 47-55.

8. The hypothesis of "recovenanting" or covenant-renewal ceremonies periodically observed in ancient Israel helps to explain both the grossly nonliterary features of the books of Moses and the vibrant sense of continuity in faith which we detect in their pages. For such a view, see A.

Weiser, *The Old Testament: Its Formation and Development* (1961), pp. 81-99, 130-135.

9. W. Zimmerli, " 'Leben' und 'Tod' im Buche des Propheten Ezechiel," *Theologische Zeitschrift*, 13 (1957), 494-508.

10. For an explication of the prophet's conception of the impending symbiotic relation between Persian empire and Israelite cult, cf. N. Gottwald, *All the Kingdoms of the Earth*, pp. 332-346.

11. C. Fritsch, *The Qumran Community, its History and Scrolls* (1956), chap. 2; G. Vermès, *Discovery in the Judean Desert* (1956), chap. 4; J. Milik, *Ten Years of Discovery in the Wilderness of Judaea*, Studies in Biblical Theology No. 26 (1957), chap. 3.

12. The following offer translations of the chief Qumran documents with introductions and notes: A. Dupont-Sommer, *The Essene Writings from Qumran* (1961); G. Vermès, *The Dead Sea Scrolls in English* (1962); T. Gaster, *The Dead Sea Scriptures* (rev. ed., 1964).

13. H. Rowley, "The Teacher of Righteousness and the Dead Sea Scrolls," *Bulletin of the John Rylands Library*, 40 (1957-58), 114-146; H. Ringgren, *The Faith of Qumran* (1961), pp. 31-43, 182-198; J. Carmignac, *Christ and the Teacher of Righteousness* (1962).

14. R. N. Flew, *Jesus and His Church* (1938); G. Johnston, *The Doctrine of the Church in the New Testament* (1943); P. Minear, *Images of the Church in the New Testament* (1960).

15. G. Vermès, *Discovery in the Judean Desert* (1956), p. 111.

16. For a catalog and brief description of chief terms and symbols for the Qumran community, see the Analytical Index in Gaster, *op. cit.*, pp. 393-401; cf. also Ringgren, *op. cit.*, pp. 201-213.

17. Manual of Discipline (IQS) iv. 17. The complicated matter of Dead Sea scroll nomenclature and abbreviations is clarified by W. Brownlee, *The Meaning of the Qumran Scrolls for the Bible* (1964), pp. xix-xxi.

18. IQS ix. 11.

19. Sometimes comparisons between the Dead Sea sect and early Christianity either have been restricted to cultic and organizational details or have been sweepingly uncritical and sensation-mongering. Among the substantive comparisons that are careful and honest are K. Stendahl, ed., *The Scrolls and the New Testament* (1961); M. Burrows, *More Light on the Dead Sea Scrolls* (1958), Part II; M. Black, *The Scrolls and Christian Origins* (1961); J. Carmignac, *Christ and the Teacher of Righteousness* (1962).

20. For the prophetic dimension in the life and teaching of Jesus, see T. Manson, *The Teaching of Jesus* (2nd ed., 1935); J. Bowman, *The Intention of Jesus* (1943), chap. 2; J. Jeremias, *Jesus' Promise to the Nations*, Studies in Biblical Theology No. 24 (1956); W. Kuemmel, *Promise and Fulfilment: the Eschatological Message of Jesus*, Studies in Biblical Theology No. 23 (1956).

# PART II

1. Three of the images examined in this part of the study are poetic. The primary members in Hebrew poetry are the half (or one-third) lines that fall into parallel with one another; taken in pairs (or sometimes in threes), they create a single thought or image usually by repetition, but also by contrast or extension. This so-called "parallelism of members" is indicated in the writer's translations by a *single diagonal* after each half or one-third line to mark the lesser stops (equivalent to a comma) and a *double diagonal* after each two or three members in parallel to mark the major stops or caesuras (equivalent to a period or semicolon). For fuller explanation and illustration of Hebrew poetics, cf. N. Gottwald, "Hebrew Poetry," *IDB*, III (1962), pp. 829-838, and G. Gray, *The Forms of Hebrew Poetry* (1915).

2. M. Buber, *Moses* (1946), especially the chapter on "Saga and History," pp. 13-19.

3. There are many valuable, but necessarily incomplete and inconclusive, contributions to a critical reconstruction of the exodus and wilderness events: B. Mazar, ed., *Views of the Biblical World*, I (1959), pp. 127-176; Y. Aharoni, "Kadesh Barnea and Mount Sinai," in *God's Wilderness*, ed. B. Rothenberg (1961), pp. 117-170; F. Cross, "The Tabernacle: A Study from an Archaeological and Historical Approach," *Biblical Archaeologist*, 10 (1947), 45-68; T. Meek, *Hebrew Origins* (rev. ed., 1950), chaps. 1-3.

4. O. Eissfeldt, *Hexateuch-Synopse* (1922), pp. 46-47; M. Newman, *The People of the Covenant* (1962), pp. 40, 46.

5. A. McNiele, *The Book of Exodus*, "Westminster Commentaries" (1908), p. xxv, states that the unit 3b-6 "appears to be a Deuteronomic expansion." M. Noth, *Exodus: A Commentary* (1962), pp. 154, 157 regards vss. 3b-9a as "a later addition to the mainly JE account of chap. 19 because it anticipates the theophany" and "contains deuteronomistic phrases particularly in vs. 5."

6. S. Driver, *An Introduction to the Literature of the Old Testament* (9th ed., 1913), pp. 32-33, conjectures that vss. 3b-9 were from J, but he thinks that vss. 4-6 were "probably expanded by the compiler of JE."

7. J. Barr, "Theophany and Anthropomorphism in the Old Testament," *Supplements to Vetus Testamentum*, VII (1960), pp. 31-38.

8. T. Meek, *Hebrew Origins* (rev. ed., 1950), chap. 2, gives a lucid and balanced comparison of Israelite and other Near Eastern laws.

9. Concerning the events of 705-701 and Isaiah's interpretations of them, see N. Gottwald, *All the Kingdoms of the Earth*, op. cit., pp. 175-196.

10. H. Wildberger, "Die Voelkerwallfahrt zum Zion, Jes. II. 1-5," *Vetus Testamentum*, 7 (1957), esp. pp. 75-76; B. Duhm, *Das Buch Jesaja*, "Handbuch zum Alten Testament" (4th ed., 1922), pp. 36-39.

11. Gottwald, *All the Kingdoms of the Earth*, pp. 196-198.
12. Gottwald, *op. cit.*, pp. 198-200.
13. R. Bainton, *Christian Attitudes toward War and Peace: A Historical Survey and Critical Re-evaluation* (1960).
14. A. Alt, "Die Rolle Samarias bei der Entstehung des Judentums," *Kleine Schriften*, II, 1934 (reprinted 1953), pp. 325-329; Gottwald, *All the Kingdoms of the Earth*, pp. 270-271, 345.
15. The formative contribution of the fall of Jerusalem in 587 B.C. to the development of the canon is argued by T. Vriezen, *An Outline of Old Testament Theology* (1958), pp. 14-15, 40-41; and to subsequent Jewish thought by N. Gottwald, *Studies in the Book of Lamentations*, "Studies in Biblical Theology No. 14" (rev. ed., 1962), chap. 3.
16. In the vast literature on the Servant, a few titles are proposed which both indicate the great range of views held by interpreters and argue their authors' own points of view: N. Gottwald, *A Light to the Nations* (1959), pp. 413-426; J. Muilenburg, *IB*, V (1956), pp. 406-414; J. Lindblom, *The Servant Songs in Deutero-Isaiah* (1951); C. North, *The Suffering Servant in Deutero-Isaiah* (rev. ed., 1956).
17. The following scholars take the position that the Servant is a composite figure reflecting Israel's religious history, with greater or less attention to the mythical ingredients of the portrait: H. Robinson, *The Cross of the Servant* (1926); O. Eissfeldt, "The Ebed-Jahwe in Isa. XL-LV in the Light of the Israelite Conception of the Community and the Individual, the Ideal and the Real," *Expository Times*, 44 (1932), 261-268; J. Muilenburg, *IB*, V (1956), pp. 408-410; O. Kaiser, *Der koenigliche Knecht. Eine traditionsgeschichtlich-exegetische Studie ueber die Ebed-Jahwe-Lieder beim Deuterojesaja* (1959). For the supporting concept more widely applied in biblical exegesis, cf. H. W. Robinson, *Corporate Personality in Ancient Israel* (Facet Books, Biblical Series 11; 1964), reprint of a 1937 essay.
18. The more traditional view of the "missionary" character of Isaiah of the exile will be found in H. Rowley, *The Missionary Message of the Old Testament* (1959), chaps. 3 and 4; countered by the "mediatorial" view of R. Martin-Achard, *A Light to the Nations: a Study of the Old Testament Conception of Israel's Mission to the World* (1962), chap. 2.
19. The fuller historical exegesis of this passage is developed in an unpublished paper by Gottwald, "Isaiah 19:16-25, Five Seventh-Century B.C. Oracles Concerning Egypt," presented to a class at Brandeis University in 1962; its argument is presented in greatly condensed form in *All the Kingdoms of the Earth*, *op. cit.*, pp. 224-228.
20. E. Meyer, *Geschichte des Altertums*, III (2nd ed., 1909), p. 146; A. Alt, *Kleine Schriften*, I (1910), p. 77; F. Kienitz, *Die politische Geschichte Aegyptens vom 7 bis zum 4 Jahrhundert vor der Zeitwende*

(1953), pp. 39-40. A related line of argument based on the Bethel cult at Elephantine is advanced by W. Albright, *Archaeology and the Religion of Israel* (3rd ed., 1953), pp. 168-175 to support the possibility that Jews were settling in Egypt as early as the last half of the seventh century.

21. E. Kissane, *The Book of Isaiah* (rev. ed., 1960), pp. 203, 210-211.
22. Gottwald, *All the Kingdoms of the Earth*, pp. 112, 117-119.
23. Gottwald, *op. cit.*, pp. 221-222.

# PART III

1. Useful data and interpretations concerning the rise of synagogue and church, and their interconnections, are found in: I. Sonne, "Synagogue," *IDB*, IV (1962), pp. 476-491; I. Elbogen, *Der juedische Gottesdienst in seiner geschichtliche Entwicklung* (3rd ed., 1931); G. Moore, *Judaism in the First Centuries of the Christian Era*, I (1927); W. Oesterley, *The Jewish Background of the Christian Liturgy* (1925); F. Foakes-Jackson and K. Lake, *The Beginnings of Christianity*, I (1933).

2. A preference is shown in this study for the term "communion" to express the relation between God and Israel or the church (cf. T. Vriezen: ". . . the covenant between God and the people did not bring these two 'partners' into a contract-relation, but into a communion, originating with God, in which Israel was bound to Him completely and made dependent on Him," *An Outline of Old Testament Theology* [1958], p. 142) but not to the exclusion of the more precise technical term "covenant," which Eichrodt prefers as "a convenient symbol for an assurance much wider in scope and controlling the formation of the national faith at its deepest level, without which Israel would not be Israel" (*Theology of the Old Testament*, I [1961], p. 14 translated from the preface to the 5th rev. ed., 1957).

3. M. Buber, *Two Types of Faith* (1951), sees Judaism as a national religion of Emunah (Trust) and Christianity as an individual religion of Pistis (Belief). They are fundamentally different in nature and origin. Yet his closing lines approach the argument of this writer: ". . . an Israel striving after the renewal of its faith through the rebirth of the person and a Christianity striving for the renewal of its faith through the rebirth of nations would have something as yet unsaid to say to each other and a help to give to one another—hardly to be conceived at the present time" (p. 174).

4. A. Nygren, *Agape and Eros* (1932-53), makes the God-originated love of the New Testament (agape) so transcendent and universal that he

is unable to find it in the man-originated, time- and space-bound love of the Old Testament (*eros*).

5. For a sketch of the older Israelite messianic views see N. Gottwald, "The Messianic Hope," *Jews and Christians: Preparation for Dialogue*, ed. G. Knight (1965), pp. 66-73; the fuller data are analyzed in markedly contrasting manners by J. Klausner, *The Messianic Idea in Israel* (1955) and S. Mowinckel, *He That Cometh* (1956).

6. O. Cullmann, *The Christology of the New Testament* (1957), gives more room to Jesus' "self-consciousness" than most recent interpreters but the content turns out to be meager apart from the effects of Jesus, for he notes: "the person must be known in the work" (p. 326); G. Bornkamm, *Jesus of Nazareth* (1959), pp. 169-178 expresses the more radical skepticism on the subject: "No customary or current conception, no title or office which Jewish tradition and expectation held in readiness, serves to authenticate his mission, or exhausts the secret of his being. It is impossible to solve the mystery with the logic, of whatever type, of any preceding doctrinal system" (p. 178).

7. On Judaism and Christianity as "sister religions" see comments of the author in *Expository Times*, 74 (1963), p. 212, and of G. Knight in *Jews and Christians: Preparation for Dialogue* (p. 179).

8. The notion of Jews and Christians as joint contributors to the *plērōma* (fullness) of God as advanced by Knight, *op. cit.*, chap. 10, moves in this direction but its implications are not carried far enough to break unequivocally with the traditional pattern of Jewish-Christian confrontation.

9. The Noachian or Noachide Laws are explained in *The Jewish Encyclopedia*, VII (1904), pp. 648-650; *The Universal Jewish Encyclopedia*, VIII (1942), pp. 227-228; K. Kohler, *Jewish Theology* (1918), pp. 48-51, 403-405, 412-413.

10. C. Dodd, "Natural Law in the New Testament," *New Testament Studies* (1953), pp. 129-142; A. Wilder, "Equivalents of Natural Law in the Teaching of Jesus," *Journal of Religion*, 26 (1946), 125-135. On John, chap. 1, see E. Hoskyns and F. Davey, *The Fourth Gospel* (1947), pp. 136-163. On Romans, chap. 2, see W. Sanday and A. Headlam, *ICC* on Romans (1895), pp. 53-62; and F. Leenhardt, *The Epistle to the Romans* (1961), pp. 80-84.

11. For an argument along this theological line, which also uses psychological and sociological analyses, see W. Watt, *Truth in the Religions* (1963), esp. chap. 8.

12. Consider, for example, the brief but unexpectedly "theological" explanation of the self-immolation of Buddhist monks contained in a letter addressed to Martin Luther King, Jr., by Thich Nhat Hanh, a Vietnamese Buddhist, "In Search of the Enemy of Man," *Fellowship* (the magazine of the Fellowship of Reconciliation), September 1965,

p. 6. Note also in the same issue comments on the relation between Vietnamese Buddhism and the war in Vietnam by Howard Schomer, member of the Fellowship's Clergymen's Emergency Committee to Visit Vietnam, in "A New Approach to Vietnam" (pp. 4-6).

13. R. Slater, *Can Christians Learn from Other Religions?* (1963).
14. Article by P. Gillon, " 'Jews of Christian Faith'—Defining Their Position," *The Jerusalem Post*, February 8, 1963.
15. A Columbia University Seminar on Inter-Religious Relations (1948-58) explored the norms which religious bodies have formulated for their members in their relations with members of other religions, both in faith and in worship, and the criticisms and rationalizations these norms are receiving in present discussions among leaders of the chief religions. The results have been published in M. Jung, S. Nikhilananda, H. Schneider, eds., *Relations among Religions Today: A Handbook of Policies and Principles* (1963).
16. "Syncretism" is used pejoratively in this book, somewhat arbitrarily, for nonorganic and intellectualistic religious composites, but it has a wide range of meanings, some of which are neutral or even positive, cf. J. Carman, "Syncretism: Historical Phenomenon and Theological Judgment," *Andover Newton Quarterly*, 4.4 (1964), 30-43.
17. S. W. Baron, *A Social and Religious History of the Jews*, II (1937), chap. 10, and *The Jewish Community*, I (1942), chaps. 6-8.
18. O. Kraines, *Government and Politics in Israel* (1961), chaps. 9-10.
19. T. M. Parker, *Christianity and the State in the Light of History* (1955), traces the history of attitudes toward church-state tensions from the biblical era through the Reformation; J. C. Bennett, *Christians and the State* (1958), presents a constructive contemporary viewpoint which reflects the long and turbulent history of the problem.
20. For the theological and ethical significance of this historico-political conception of God and man, see N. Gottwald, *All the Kingdoms of the Earth*, chap. 5.
21. O. Cullmann, *The State in the New Testament* (1956), gives a much greater political significance to the teachings and actions of Jesus than do most interpreters.
22. J. Jeremias, *Jesus' Promise to the Nations* (1956).
23. The ways in which wisdom and prophetic elements markedly qualify the apocalyptic features of the Gospels are effectively shown by J. Bowman, *The Intention of Jesus* (1943); A. Wilder, *Eschatology and Ethics in the Teaching of Jesus* (rev. ed., 1950); H. Windisch, *The Meaning of the Sermon on the Mount* (1951 trans. of 1937 rev. ed.).
24. N. Gottwald, "Prophetic Faith and Contemporary International Relation," *Biblical Realism Confronts the Nation*, ed. P. Peachey (1963), pp. 68-87.
25. L. Ebersole, *Church Lobbying in the Nation's Capital* (1951).
26. The theological relevance of the pragmatic team approach to problem-

solving is explored by H. Cox, *The Secular City* (1965), pp. 60-70, 105-123, 173-191, 263-265.

27. A. F. Geyer, *Piety and Politics: American Protestantism in the World Arena* (1963).

28. R. W. Spike, *The Freedom Revolution and the Churches* (1965).

29. Attributed to Milton Meyer in R. T. Templin, *Democracy and Non-violence: The Role of the Individual in World Crisis* (1965), p. 284.

30. W. Miller, *Nonviolence: A Christian Interpretation* (1964), is a detailed, cautious, but hopeful exploration of the possibilities of non-violent resistance in international affairs. His survey of some historic cases of successful nonviolence between nations is of particular interest. He gives good reasons for believing that both the East German and Hungarian revolts against communist regimes would have come nearer to succeeding had the rebels been trained in a nonviolent discipline.

31. A detailed and devastating documentation of this thesis is Robert Scheer, *How the United States Got Involved in Vietnam* (A Report to the Center for the Study of Democratic Institutions; July 1965). See also J. Lacouture, *Vietnam: Between Two Truces* (1966).

32. See especially the searching comparison of Algeria and Vietnam by a Pakistani sympathetic to the United States, E. Ahmad, "Revolutionary Warfare," in *Vietnam: History, Documents, and Opinions on a Major World Crisis* (ed. M. Gettleman) (1965), pp. 351-62.

33. Some of the following paragraphs on the nature of the church have been drawn either verbatim, or with revision, from a report submitted for the National Theological Conference of the American Baptist Convention held in Green Lake, Wisconsin, July 6-11, 1959, on "Ecclesiology." The portions extracted or revised were originally my own, as chairman-writer, but the ideas and the wording were thoroughly discussed and finally achieved the status of consensus in our report. I therefore acknowledge the contributions of my fellow study-group members: John W. Brush, Lee Keck, Roger Nicole, Spencer Parsons, Ralph Reynolds, Homer L. Trickett.

34. These nuances in the Reformers' views of the church as visible and invisible are drawn from Herman Bavinck, *Gereformeerde Dogmatik*, II (2nd ed., 1912), pp. 309-313, as translated and reported to the writer by Roger Nicole.

35. Cf. the highly perceptive essay by G. Ebeling, "The Significance of the Critical Historical Method for Church and Theology in Protestantism," *Word and Faith* (1960), pp. 17-61. Ebeling notes that "a mere refurbishing and repetition of the theology of the Reformers is as utterly impossible as the by-passing of the intervening history with its alterations in the statement of the problems and its new presentations of them" (p. 18).

36. An essentially organic view of the church, stressing its historical continuity and precariousness as well as its mixed sociotheological character,

178

was advanced by H. R. Niebuhr, *The Meaning of Revelation* (1941), and elaborated on its cultural side in *Christ and Culture* (1951). J. Gustafson, *Treasure in Earthen Vessels* (1961), has made superb use of social theory to analyze the church as community, and C. Welch, *The Reality of the Church* (1958) has developed a similar view on the theological side in relation to several major Christian doctrines.

37. See Cox, *op. cit.*, chaps. 5-6.
38. Mihajlo Mihajlov, in *The New Leader*, August 30, 1965.
39. Articles by Santiago Alvares and Libero Pierantozzi in *The World Marxist Review* as reported in an article by Colin Legum in the (London) *Observer* and reprinted in *San Francisco Chronicle*, August 29, 1965.
40. H. R. Niebuhr, *Christ and Culture* (1951), p. 104.

# SUGGESTED READING

## The Old Testament:

Buber, M., *Moses*, 1946.

Eichrodt, W., *Theology of the Old Testament*, I, 1961; II, 1967.

Gottwald, N., *All the Kingdoms of the Earth. Israelite Prophecy and International Relations in the Ancient Near East*, 1964.

——, *A Light to the Nations: An Introduction to the Old Testament*, 1959.

Heschel, A., *The Prophets*, 1962.

Lindblom, J., *Prophecy in Ancient Israel*, 1962.

——, *The Servant Songs in Deutero-Isaiah*, 1951.

Martin-Achard, R., *A Light to the Nations: A Study of the Old Testament Conception of Israel's Mission to the World*, 1962.

McCarthy, D., *Treaty and Covenant*, 1963.

Meek, T., *Hebrew Origins*, rev. ed., 1950.

Mendenhall, G., *Law and Covenant in Israel and in the Ancient Near East*, 1955.

Mowinckel, S., *He That Cometh*, 1956.

Napier, B., *Prophets in Perspective*, 1962.

Newman, M., *The People of the Covenant*, 1962.

North, C., *The Suffering Servant in Deutero-Isaiah*, rev. ed., 1956.

Rowley, H., *The Missionary Message of the Old Testament*, 1959.

## Dead Sea Scrolls:

Black, M., *The Scrolls and Christian Origins*, 1961.

Brownlee, W., *The Meaning of the Qumran Scrolls for the Bible*, 1964.

Carmignac, J., *Christ and the Teacher of Righteousness*, 1962.

Dupont-Sommer, A., *The Essene Writings from Qumran*, 1961.

Fritsch, C., *The Qumran Community, Its History and Scrolls*, 1956.

Gaster, T., *The Dead Sea Scriptures*, rev. ed., 1964.

Ringgren, H., *The Faith of Qumran*, 1961.

Stendahl, K., ed., *The Scrolls and the New Testament*, 1961.

Vermès, G., *The Dead Sea Scrolls in English*, 1962.

——, *Discovery in the Judean Desert*, 1956.

### The New Testament:

Bornkamm, G., *Jesus of Nazareth*, 1959.

Bowman, J., *The Intention of Jesus*, 1943.

Cullmann, O., *The Christology of the New Testament*, 1957.

Flew, R., *Jesus and His Church*, 1938.

Jeremias, J., *Jesus' Promise to the Nations*, 1956.

Johnston, G., *The Doctrine of the Church in the New Testament*, 1943.

Kuemmel, W., *Promise and Fulfilment: The Eschatological Message of Jesus*, 1956.

Manson, T., *The Teaching of Jesus*, 2nd ed., 1935.

Minear, P., *Images of the Church in the New Testament*, 1960.

Wilder, A., *Eschatology and Ethics in the Teaching of Jesus*, rev. ed., 1950.

### The Church in Its Jewish and Christian Forms:

Baron, S., *A Social and Religious History of the Jews*, II, 1937.

——, *The Jewish Community*, I, 1942.

Baum, G., *The Jews and the Gospel, a Re-examination of the New Testament*, 1961.

Buber, M., *Two Types of Faith*, 1951.

Foakes-Jackson, F., and Lake, M., *The Beginnings of Christianity*, I, 1933.

Gilbert, A., *A Jew in Christian America*, 1966.

Knight, G., ed., *Jews and Christians: Preparation for Dialogue*, 1965.

Moore, G., *Judaism in the First Centuries of the Christian Era*, I, 1927.

Oesterley, W., *The Jewish Background of the Christian Liturgy*, 1925.

Scharper, P., ed., *Torah and Gospel: Jewish and Catholic Theology in Dialogue*, 1966.

## The Church and Nonhistorical Religions:

Anderson, G., ed., *The Theology of the Christian Mission*, 1961.

Blauw, J., *The Missionary Nature of the Church. A Survey of the Biblical Theology of Mission*, 1962.

Jung, M., et al., eds., *Relations among Religions Today: A Handbook of Policies and Principles*, 1963.

Kraemer, H., *The Christian Message in a Non-Christian World*, 1938.

Lamott, W., *Revolution in Missions*, 1954.

Slater, R., *Can Christians Learn from Other Religions?* 1963.

———, *World Religions and World Community*, 1963.

Soper, E., *The Philosophy of the Christian World Mission*, 1943.

Tillich, P., *Christianity and the Encounter of the World Religions*, 1961.

Van Leeuwen, A., *Christianity and World History*, 1964.

Watt, W., *Truth in the Religions*, 1963.

## The Church and the Nations:

Bainton, R., *Christian Attitudes toward War and Peace*, 1960.

Bennett, J., *Christians and the State*, 1958.

———, *Foreign Policy in Christian Perspective*, 1966.

Cullmann, O., *The State in the New Testament*, 1956.

Ebersole, L., *Church Lobbying in the Nation's Capital*, 1951.

Gettleman, M., ed., *Vietnam: History, Documents, and Opinions on a Major World Crisis*, 1965.

Geyer, A., *Piety and Politics: American Protestantism in the World Arena*, 1963.

Lacouture, J., *Vietnam: Between Two Truces*, 1966.

Miller, W., *Nonviolence: A Christian Interpretation*, 1964.

Parker, T., *Christianity and the State in the Light of History*, 1955.

Spike, R., *The Freedom Revolution and the Churches*, 1965.

Templin, R., *Democracy and Non-violence: The Role of the Individual in World Crisis*, 1965.

## Church and Culture:

Altizer, T., and Hamilton, W., *Radical Theology and the Death of God*, 1966.

Bonhoeffer, D., *Letters and Papers from Prison*, 1962.

Cox, H., *The Secular City*, 1965.

Dubay, W., *The Human Church*, 1966.

Gilkey, L., *How the Church Can Minister to the World without Losing Itself*, 1964.

Gustafson, J., *Treasure in Earthen Vessels*, 1961.

Jacobs, P., and Landau, S., eds., *The New Radicals*, 1966.

Newfield, J., *A Prophetic Minority*, 1966.

Niebuhr, H. R., *Christ and Culture*, 1951.

——, *The Meaning of Revelation*, 1941.

Nygren, A., *Agape and Eros*, 1932–1953.

Van Buren, P., *The Secular Meaning of the Gospel*, 1963.

Welch, C., *The Reality of the Church*, 1958.

# Index of Biblical Passages

# Subject Index

187